Int~~roduction~~

The Brecon Beacons Nati~~onal Park~~ ...der to the Tywi valley in Carmarthensh~~ire~~ ...an area of 520 square miles. This swathe of so~~...~~ ...as of high ground by the rivers Usk, Taf and ...ic infancy, descend to meet the salt water of ...des of the south, Newport, Cardiff and Swans~~ea~~ ...~~respecti~~vely. At the eastern extremity the Black Mountains (plural) rise up steeply from the English midlands. To the west, the eponymous Black Mountain (singular) covers a vast expanse of remote and lonely moorland beyond the sources of the Tawe and Usk. This book covers the two intervening mountain blocks – the 'Central' Beacons and Fforest Fawr. Another Kittiwake guide covers the Black Mountains.

Strictly speaking the term 'Brecon Beacons' applies to the three or four highest peaks a few miles south of Brecon, crowned by Pen y Fan. At 886 metres its distinctive cap is the highest land in southern Britain and only just fails to break through the magic *3000 feet* mark.

The Central Beacons and Fforest Fawr share geological features. The northern moors and escarpments expose red sandstone. In the Beacons, this culminates in the distinctive sloping plateaux on the summits of Corn Du and Pen y Fan, presiding over the Usk valley and hills of mid Wales beyond (**Walks 15–18**). In Fforest Fawr, the spectacular, hidden alpine cliffs of Craig Cerrig-gleisiad and Craig Cwm-du also look northwards (**Walks 19–20**). However, in the south, limestone comes to the surface and gives an entirely different character to the topography and fauna. These porous rocks gestate the young Taf Fechan (**Walk 6**) and Nedd Fechan. The latter, with its tributaries, has carved dramatic gorges and spectacular waterfalls (**Walks 12–14**). Swansea's river, the Tawe, also crosses limestone and its upper valley hides the biggest cave system in Wales (**Walk 11**). There are many other highlights to visit, including the country's second largest lake at Llangors (**Walk 1**) and the impressive limestone quarries at Mynydd Llangatwg (**Walk 7**). A number of walks enjoy a section on the tranquil Brecon and Monmouthshire Canal (**Walks 6, 7, 9**), visit Iron Age forts (**Walks 3 & 6**), follow forest trails (**Walks 5 & 8**) or discover a steam railway (**Walk 10**). A great starting point for new or regular visitors is the National Park's Mountain Centre just south of Brecon (**Walks 3, 4, 20**).

Walks in this book vary from 3 to over 10 miles. Some are relatively gentle strolls and others are serious mountain expeditions. Weather makes a huge difference to the seriousness of a walk in this upland region. Conditions change quickly so please take care and keep safe. The 'strenuous' walks (**15–20**) all require mountain precautions (though in some cases there are shorter alternatives for poor weather). Take extra food, drinks, spare clothing and waterproofs. Also carry a first aid kit and an emergency 'bivvy' bag. Take and use a large-scale map to supplement the maps in this book.

This is a wonderful area to walk, with a huge variety of scenery and much of interest. Enjoy it!

A STROLL AROUND LLANGORS LAKE

DESCRIPTION This is the easiest walk in the book; a pleasant 3-mile stroll on a summer evening. Llangors Lake is the largest natural stretch of water in southern Wales. Access to the lakeshore is generally poor, which is frustrating to walkers but helps to protect the remarkable natural environment and habitat. This walk is the best way of gaining some intimacy with the water's edge and marshes that surround it. The path follows the shoreline at a discrete distance, offering good opportunities to observe birds and to study the plant life of the marsh. It can be flooded after wet weather. Llangors Lake, or Llyn Syfaddan, is not only a wildlife sanctuary. It also has a long historical pedigree, with the remains of an ancient lake settlement overlooked by an Iron Age fort.

START Car park, Llangors Common. SO 129273.

DIRECTIONS To reach Llangors, use the B4560 between Talgarth and Bwlch. Follow the signs from Llangors village to the lake. There is a large area of common land and parking is available here. Llangors is not easy to reach by public transport.

I From the car park, cross the access road and take the grass path directly across Llangors Common. Aim for a footbridge at the far side of the common. This crosses the Afon Llynfi. Go through the gate and BEAR LEFT following the waymark, crossing the next field diagonally. *The tops of Pen y Fan and Cribyn dominate the western horizon.* Go through the kissing gate at the end of the field and continue in the same direction across the next enclosure, a patch of reeds on the left concealing the lake. Pass through another gate and admire two ancient gnarled oak trees in the next field. Just beyond them, go through a further gate and cross a footbridge over a ditch.

2 At the other side BEAR LEFT across a water meadow. *The path is firm but yellow flag iris and reeds indicate the aqueous terrain on the fringe of the lake. The path takes a slightly elevated position in the next field, offering views across the water back to the jetty and crannog, the remains of an artificial island. At the top of the field, admire Tymawr farmhouse, which appears on maps as early as 1584.* Soon you enter Llangasty Nature Reserve. The reserve is owned by the National Park, and run by the local wildlife trust. A path to the right leads down to a hide on the lakeshore. If you have time, you can observe the birds and wildlife on the lake. Continue back on the path above a copse with duckboards now aiding the way in damper places. *Up to your right on the nearest hilltop you can see the remains of Allt yr Esgair, an Iron Age fort dating from 100CE.* The path traverses a small wood and a series of fields to arrive on a lane in front of Llangasty-Talyllyn church.

3 TURN RIGHT to look at the church, or LEFT to the lakeshore. There are various paths around the area suggesting a circular return can be made to Llangors Common. In reality, most are difficult to follow, or overgrown. The best idea is to return the way you have come, enjoying views and perspectives in the opposite direction.

Llangors Lake

Covering an area of over 150 hectares, Llangors is the second largest sheet of natural water in Wales, after Llyn Tegid near Bala. It is surrounded by a further 10 hectares of wetland and marsh and fringed by gently shelving shores. Because of these important characteristics, the lake and its surrounds are designated as a site of special scientific interest. On the edge of the water, there are beds of reeds, sedges and rushes. Alder, willow and hazel colonise the water margins. Water lilies can grow in deeper water. Insects and plants thrive here and the lake is a good habitat for dragonflies. It provides an important breeding site for reed warblers and hosts around 20 species of birds during winter including teal, pochard and tufted duck. There are substantial threats to the

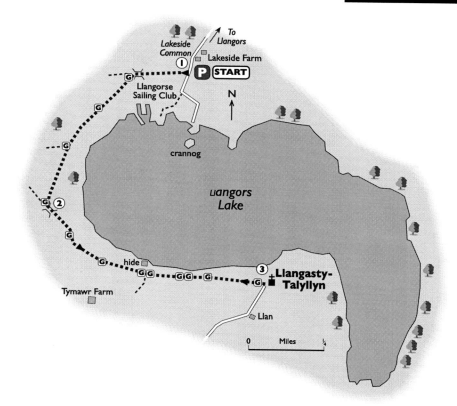

environment here, including pollution from neighbouring land and the use of the lake for boats.

The Crannog

In 1868, the remains of a crannog, or artificial island, were discovered in the lake, near the slipway on the northern shore. This may have been built as a fortified palace and would probably have supported a few buildings. Giraldus Cambriensis (Gerald of Wales), who toured Wales recruiting soldiers for the crusades in the twelfth century, recounted a legend that a city lay beneath the water.

Llangasty-Talyllyn

The church at Llangasty-Talyllyn is the only dedication to St Gastyn in the world. He was probably one of the Celtic Christians who preserved the faith during the inundation of

pagan invaders in the fifth and sixth centuries. The existence of a church here dates back many centuries. During the nineteenth century, it was substantially rebuilt as part of the high church Tractarian movement.

Llangors Lake

BRECON AND ITS SURROUNDINGS

DESCRIPTION A 6-mile tour of Brecon's environs, divided into two distinct parts. The first section leaves the town on the canal towpath to reach Brynich locks and the village of Groesffordd. It returns along a bridleway over a hill to the north of the town, crowned by an ancient fort. This section ends at point 4, and you could return directly to the town centre if you prefer. The second section loops north to follow the wooded valley of the Honddu back into the centre of town, finishing under the cathedral's rocky knoll. Allow time to enjoy a look round Brecon, a historic market town at the heart of the National Park.

A shorter alternative to this walk is a stroll along Brecon's 'Promenade', a waterside footpath at the western end of the town. To find this, follow Ship Street from the town centre until just before it crosses the Usk. TURN RIGHT here, cross the River Honddu and find the riverside path on your left. The path continues beyond the town, 1½ miles to Fenni-fach.

START Pay and display car park at Brecon Marina, SO 047283. There are several other convenient car parks in the town.

DIRECTIONS Brecon straddles the old A40, the Fishguard to London trunk road, though the town now benefits from a by-pass. The walk starts at the marina, at the western end of the Brecon and Monmouthshire Canal. It finishes at the cathedral, a short distance away on the other side of the town centre.

If using public transport, there are regular weekday bus services to Brecon from Abergavenny, Merthyr, Cardiff, Llandovery, Hay, Hereford, Builth and Newtown. On Sundays and bank holidays during the summer months, Brecon is the hub of the Beacons Bus network organised by the National Park Authority.

1 FOLLOW THE CANAL TOWPATH from the marina. The path also forms the Taff Trail, a 58-mile long distance route to Cardiff, so the route is shared with cyclists here. It is a pleasant promenade alongside the water. At the edge of the town, pass under the A40. *The traffic noise now subsides. The Usk meanders along in the next field and there are excellent views across the river to the high peaks of the Beacons. A little further on a finger post points an alternative route back to Brecon via the riverside if time is short.*

2 You soon arrive at Brynich lock. Go through the gate onto the road beyond, taking care of any traffic. *You may want to continue along the canal a little further to view the aqueduct over the Usk.* Otherwise, TURN LEFT here and follow the road under the A40 dual carriageway and on towards Groesffordd. *There is no alternative to this short section of road walking, but once you have passed under the trunk road, noise abates and it becomes a small lane. The Three Horseshoes pub lies a short way up a side turning on your right and may be a convenient refreshment stop. Just above this is the site of Groesffordd halt on the Brecon and Merthyr railway line. The line and station were closed in the early 1960s (see* **Walk 8***).* Continue on past the village, keeping straight ahead until you reach the youth hostel at Ty'n-y-caeau.

3 Just past the hostel TURN LEFT to follow a bridleway sign. Almost immediately you cross the A470. Take care here; it is a busy road. On the opposite side, the bridleway continues across a wooden footbridge and into a green lane. The route may be muddy in places but a profusion of wild flowers is a digression from sticky boots. The way improves as you approach Slwch Farm. Pass through the yard and continue along the lane on the opposite side. As the track reaches its summit, views open out to the north and you can see the remains of Slwch Tump hill fort crowning the field to your left. A public footpath to the left can reach this site, probably an Iron Age tribal centre. Pass a mast on your right and then descend to a main road on the outskirts of Brecon.

4 If you want to return directly to the town centre, turn left here. Otherwise, CROSS

THE MAIN ROAD carefully and continue straight ahead down the residential road marked by 'no entry' signs. This curves down to a small crossroads. TURN RIGHT here up the 'no through road' that soon becomes a tarmac footpath.

To the right are the playing fields of Brecon High School. Just after some small ponds, the path veers right into the school buildings. Instead, CARRY STRAIGHT ON along the grassy swathe to the left of the all-weather pitches. Keep along the side of the fields, curving round to the right until you reach a kissing gate. This gives access to the road.

5 TURN LEFT and follow the road for about 50 yards, taking care, as there is no footpath. Then TURN SHARP RIGHT down a lane signed to Forge Bridge. *You can now see the River Honddu below, which gives Brecon its Welsh name, Aberhonddu.* Just past the large white house, Forge Cottage, TURN LEFT, following a sign to Priory Groves. Cross the footbridge and TURN LEFT, now signed to Brecon. Now keep to the path nearest to the river as it passes through the wooded valley back to Brecon. As the path comes into the town, you meet a tarmac path and the cathedral lies ahead of you on a rock above the river.

6 TURN SHARP RIGHT here to climb up to it and the finish of the walk. To return straight to the town centre, BEAR LEFT.

Brecon

Brecon is a historic and attractive town. It bridges the river Usk at its confluence with the Honddu, on a strategic route to and from western Wales. The Romans built a fort just west of here at Cicucium as a staging post on their road between Gloucester and Carmarthen. Still today, Brecon is home to the South Wales Borderers, maintaining the town's military heritage through their barracks and museum. The cathedral for the diocese of Swansea and Brecon is situated on a hill just above the town centre. Originally the church of a Benedictine Priory, it became the town's parish church after the dissolution of the monasteries in the 1530s and was made a cathedral in 1923. A neighbouring sixteenth century tithe barn houses a heritage centre that interprets the history and work of the cathedral. The main west Wales trunk road passes between these mountain wildernesses, following the Usk valley. In the heart of such a rural landscape, Brecon is an important agricultural centre. Its townscape includes many Georgian buildings as well as some tasteful newer developments, including the terminal basin on the Monmouthshire and Brecon Canal.

EXPLORING AROUND THE MOUNTAIN CENTRE

DESCRIPTION Walks 3 & 4 are both 3 miles long and offer interesting and gentle excursions around the common land surrounding the National Park Authority's Visitor Centre. **Walk 3** explores the heathland northeast of the centre, culminating at the remains of an Iron Age fort overlooking the Usk valley. **Walk 4** heads west, offering extensive views from the old quarry on Allt Lom before crossing Traeth Moor nature reserve and the line of Sarn Helen, a Roman road. The Mountain Centre itself is a great focus for a visit. It offers interpretative displays and a video presentation about the national park, as well as a shop, information centre and excellent café. The lawns outside provide a grassy terrace to enjoy spectacular views of the Beacons. **Walk 20** is a longer walk from here to Fan Frynych.

START Brecon Beacons National Park Mountain Centre, near Libanus. SN 978263.

DIRECTIONS The Visitor Centre is reached by a minor road from the A470 at Libanus, about four miles south of Brecon. It is well signposted. Beacons Bus serves the centre on summer Sundays and bank holidays. Otherwise, Bus X43 (Abergavenny – Brecon – Merthyr) stops at Tai'r Bull on the main road. From here a lane and track lead to the Mountain Centre a mile away.

WALK 3
MYNYDD ILLTUD AND
TWYN Y GAER

I Go through the gate at the far end of the car park to gain access on to the common. FOLLOW THE MAIN TRACK ahead northeastwards and enjoy views right to Pen y Fan and ahead to the Black Mountains. After a while the track passes just above a small marshy pond and soon you come to a minor road. Cross this, carrying STRAIGHT AHEAD on the bridleway. You can now see the trig

point crowning Twyn y Gaer ahead. Another side road is crossed and you take the direct grassy route straight up to the Iron Age fort ahead. *Remains of the ditches are still evident and, although the ascent from this side is gentle, once at the top you realise why the fort was established here. In front of you the ground drops steeply away into the Usk valley, a key route to and from western Wales.*

2 You can vary your return by FOLLOWING THE PATH JUST TO THE LEFT of your ascent. This curves back round to re-cross the road. Here, follow the bridleway sign towards the Mountain centre. But, after a few yards, instead of continuing on this, VEER RIGHT to keep on the track next to the wall. Follow the boundary of the common all the way round until you come to a farm access road. (It is also possible to cut across the common directly back to the Mountain Centre at many points.)

3 When you reach the farm access track, TURN LEFT along it, cross the road and follow the green track back to the Mountain Centre.

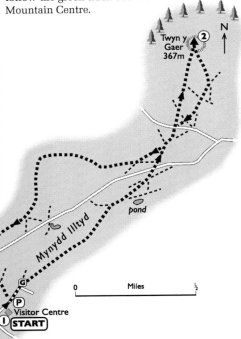

6

WALK 4
ALLT LOM AND
TRAETH MOOR

1 From the centre, walk back along the approach road to its junction with the lane. TURN RIGHT (west) and follow the road as it leaves the common over a cattle grid. *Opposite the farm there is an old graveyard in the trees. Its circular shape suggests it may have been a holy site before the arrival of Christianity.* The road leaves the enclosure and returns to the common over another cattle grid. At a T-junction, CARRY STRAIGHT ON. There are a number of tracks. Follow the one NEXT TO THE WALL. *After 200 yards, a gate in the wall indicates the point where the line of the Roman road, Sarn Helen, crosses the track. There is no obvious trace of this antiquity today.* Continue ahead, with the wall on your right. You soon come to a line of beech trees and the craggy remains of an old quarry.

2 An easy and grassy climb to the top is rewarded with excellent views. Carry straight on over it. Just beyond the quarry TURN LEFT along a green track through the gorse. In 100 yards this meets a rutted track in front of a fence. TURN LEFT along this, with the high peaks of the Beacons now directly ahead. Where the cinder path veers to the left, choose the alternative grassy FORK TO THE RIGHT. This accompanies the fence and drops gently down, crossing a farm access lane before joining a minor road. *As you* near the road, you pick up the line of Sarn Helen again. The Roman road continued in the direction of a modern pipeline marker, but again there is little in the way of obvious archaeology to evidence this important historic route. TURN RIGHT along the road.

3 Just beyond a couple more pipeline markers and about 100 yards short of a pond, TURN SHARP LEFT along an earthen track to cross the Traeth Moor nature reserve. This is an important peat wetland habitat. At the far side of the moor, join another track in front of the boundary fence. This is also the course of **Walk 20**. TURN LEFT along this back to the Mountain Centre.

The Visitor Centre

CWMTAF FOREST AND LLWYN-ON RESERVOIR

DESCRIPTION A 4½-mile tour of Cwmtaf Forest, using woodland tracks with easy gradients. The visitor centre at Garwnant offers a café, information and toilets. There is also a children's playground and a series of waymarked paths and cycle routes. This walk follows a modified version of one of the cycle routes. Small brown markers indicate the cycle route. Multi-use paths always require care, but the track is quiet and you are generally unlikely to encounter more than an occasional dog walker (and dog). Except for the last avoidable short cut path, the whole route is accessible for wheelchairs and pushchairs. The return leg includes a section along the access road from Llwyn-on dam.

START The Garwnant Forest Visitor Centre. SO 003131.

DIRECTIONS Garwnant is the centre for Cwmtaf woodlands. An approach road leads from the A470 Merthyr – Brecon road, five miles north of Merthyr. Parking is available at the centre (fee payable).

Bus X43 (Abergavenny – Brecon – Merthyr) passes the access road on the A470 (Mondays – Saturdays). On summer Sundays and bank holidays some Beacons bus services call at the visitor centre itself.

From the parking area, WALK BACK DOWN THE APPROACH ROAD for a few yards. Where it bends to the left by a couple of disabled parking spaces, TURN RIGHT and follow the cycle and footpath waymarks along a forest road. Pass the barrier and almost immediately BEAR LEFT to follow the footpath instead of the track. There is a stream just down to the left and some duckboards offer the opportunity to explore a pond and marshy area. The footpath soon crosses a bridge and then TURNS LEFT at a blue way mark. Climb gently up through the woods to meet a forest track.

2 TURN LEFT and follow this track as it descends gently through the forest. After a while the trees thin out and there are good views over Llwyn-on reservoir. After a right hand bend the track now climbs gradually. Ignore a left hand branch and continue following occasional brown cycle track signs. The track curves to the right and then comes to a junction. TURN SHARP LEFT here (waymark). The gradual ascent continues. After another 400 yards or so, TURN LEFT at another slate sign and way mark.

3 CROSS A MINOR ROAD at Pen-yr-heol and continue with the track on the opposite side. A little later the track bends left and you soon come to a junction. TURN LEFT, following the signs. Now the path continues to descend and the views open out over the reservoir and back over the highest Beacons. Eventually it reaches the reservoir access road.

4 TURN LEFT to follow this road, also part of the Taff Trail, a long distance walking and cycling route from Cardiff to Brecon. It is a quiet access lane, but there is still some traffic, especially on summer weekends or during holiday periods, so take care. Unfortunately access to the shoreline is restricted to permit holders with fishing rods. Nevertheless, the views across the water are picturesque.

5 As you approach the head of the reservoir, immediately after crossing a stream, there is a green post marked with 'H9' and decorated with red and white tape. TURN LEFT up a footpath here. This leads back through the woods a short distance to the car park and visitor centre.

Llwyn-on reservoir
Llwyn-on reservoir was built by Cardiff Corporation and opened in 1926. It is one of three reservoirs in this valley serving Wales' capital city and has a capacity of 5.5 million litres. A plaque on the left also helpfully reminds you that the average rainfall here is 67 inches a year.

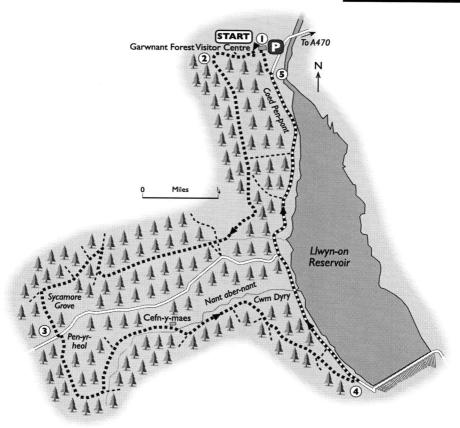

Taff Trail

The Taff Trail is now a long distance walking and cycling route between Cardiff and Brecon. It is also encountered on **Walks 8** and **10**.

Llwyn-on Reservoir

CWM TAF FECHAN AND VAYNOR CHURCH

DESCRIPTION Starting at the mansion home of one of South Wales' most successful nineteenth century ironmasters, this easy 6-mile walk encounters the dramatic gorge of the Taf Fechan. This peaceful and attractive limestone nature reserve is just minutes from Merthyr Tydfil, once Wales' largest town. The route epitomises the close interface between the great natural beauty of the Welsh valleys and the industrial exploitation of these resources. Take time to explore the museum and grounds at Cyfarthfa to get a feel for the history and resilience of this place and its people.

START Cyfarthfa Castle, Merthyr Tydfil. SO 042073.

DIRECTIONS Cyfarthfa Castle is a mile north of the centre of Merthyr, on the road towards Cefn-coed-y-cymmer. From the A470 follow the signs to Cefn-coed-y-cymmer..

There are frequent buses from Merthyr bus station to the park gates. Take the Trefechan or Pontsticill services. Bus X43 runs every two hours from Abergavenny via Brecon, passing Cyfarthfa's gates.

I From the front of the building, take the park access road north (LEFT as you face the doors to the castle) to the park's Cefn gates. Go through the great iron gateway and TURN LEFT. Almost immediately come to the main road. TURN RIGHT alongside this. Straight away you pass the sign for Cefn-coed-y-cymmer and the road bears left crossing a bridge high above the Taf Fechan. The footpath begins under this bridge, but the legal access is not as awkward as it may appear! To get down there, immediately after the bridge and opposite a building engraved with the title 'Gwynne's Arms', TURN RIGHT down a driveway. Re-cross the river on the old bridge and KEEP RIGHT in front of the house, following a path to the right of the garage, which descends under the road bridge. *This is not the most salubrious of locations, but it is quickly left behind.* Follow the steps down to the RIGHT to join the riverside path. TURN RIGHT to follow this public footpath. Stone setts indicate the path was once a tramway. Now nature has reclaimed it. You may see dippers and speckled wood butterflies. Soon you pass under the graceful modern arch of the Heads of the Valleys Road and more open country begins. *The source of the water for Cyfarthfa's lake is now revealed, a feeder from the Taf Fechan. This supplied the local iron works with water needed to power the machinery. It still carries water to Cyfarthfa Park's ornamental lake, which was used a reservoir of extra water for the iron works during any period of drought.*

2 A gate takes you into a delightful limestone meadow and marks the entrance to Cwm Taf Fechan Nature Reserve. A footbridge leads to an alternative footpath on the other side. *However, stay on this side for now and enjoy the primroses and violets if you're walking in spring, shortly passing the sluice for the feeder.* The path climbs gradually beside the river as it tumbles down a series of rapids carving its way through rocky limestone crags. *The woodland is now more mature and is home to a variety of bird species such as woodpeckers, wrens and dippers. The woodland gives way to a meadow before you climb a stepped path to the nature reserve car park at Pont Sarn. Morlais Castle stood high on the limestone above here. The Lord of Glamorgan built it in about 1270. Little remains today. The cliffs were quarried to provide lime for Dowlais iron works.*

3 TURN LEFT down the road and cross Pont Sarn. A Roman road crossed the river at this point on its way north from Cardiff. Immediately after the bridge, TURN RIGHT to enter the National Park by a sign for Pont Sarn. *The footpath soon passes under a magnificent viaduct built in 1865 to carry the Brecon to Merthyr railway. It now carries the traffic free Taff Trail. It is 455 feet long and 92 feet high.* A stile leads to a boggy area, where marsh marigolds have taken full advantage of the terrain. Duckboards aid progress on the rocky side of the ravine. After a while another stile leads to a clearing next to a footbridge. At this point TURN LEFT, away from the river, and climb the path up the grassy bank to a stile. *Pass a house, the Church Tavern, which dates from the seventeenth century. It was once a court, and more recently a pub. Just past it, arrive at Vaynor church.*

4 *The church was built in 1870, through the generosity of Robert Crawshay, of Merthyr's iron making dynasty. His munificence was however conditional on Vaynor's own congregation. They were to help the poorer parishioners of nearby Cefn-coed build a church for the area's burgeoning population.* Just past the church follow the green lane leading off. It soon passes the original church, now in ruins amidst an overgrown graveyard. *This dates back to 1295, though a church may have been here since the eighth century.* Cross the footbridge and continue along the lane until it meets a road. An odd Hispanic looking building lies just to the right, graced by the name of 'Hy Brasail'. However, we TURN LEFT here and follow the road a short distance to the old Pont Sarn Inn.

5 From the car park opposite, you can gain access to the Taff Trail that you have just crossed on a road bridge. Follow the Taff Trail LEFT (towards Merthyr). This is a high level route, a contrast to the outward journey deep in the valley. Progress is quick on this level, well-surfaced route. Remember it is also a cycle route. *Further on there are good views of the viaduct carrying the Heads*

of the Valleys road over the Taf Fechan gorge. The Trail itself now crosses the main road on a humbler steel bridge and comes to an end. Follow the sign down a path by St John's Church, Cefn-coed and along a side street to the main road. TURN LEFT here to follow Cefn's High Street back to Cyfarthfa.

Cyfarthfa Castle

Cyfarthfa is actually a 'mock castle', built by William Crawshay as a family home in the early nineteenth century. The mansion was surrounded by parkland and overlooked his ironworks. Crawshay was one of the leading industrial entrepreneurs in south Wales. Iron made Merthyr into the biggest town in Wales during the Victorian period. The town was also a cauldron for radical non-conformity and political reform. Today, Cyfarthfa is owned by Merthyr Council and is open daily as a museum. Entrance is free. There is also a tearoom and a museum shop. The grounds are open from early morning until dusk and there is ample free car parking.

11

LLANGATWG QUARRIES AND CRAIG Y CILAU

DESCRIPTION Climbing from the Usk to the dramatic limestone cliffs of Mynydd Llangatwg, this 6-mile walk provides a great variety of scenery from wooded towpath to limestone heath. It explores the impressive National nature Reserve at Craig y Cilau and offers great views across the Usk valley.

START Car Park, near the parish church in Llangattock village. SO 210178.

DIRECTIONS Llangattock lies on the southern bank of the Usk, opposite Crickhowell, which sits astride the A40 between Abergavenny and Brecon. The village can be reached from Crickhowell across the town's historic bridge, which is guarded by a set of very slow three-way traffic lights. Alternatively, you can get to Llangattock from Gilwern by the A4077. The village's car park is convenient but not well signposted. Using the tower as a landmark, find the parish church. The car park is behind a wall opposite the church. However, to reach it by car you have to continue on left past the church until a 'P' sign points through a small housing estate.

Nearest public transport is at Crickhowell (½ mile) – bus service X43 to Abergavenny and Brecon runs Mondays to Saturdays. Beacons Bus serves the town on summer Sundays and bank holidays.

I LEAVE THE CAR PARK THROUGH THE GAP in the wall opposite the church. *Just to your left is a water trough set in the wall. A plaque indicates it was installed at the expense of GFW Miles Esq. of Llangattock Park in 1881, alongside a quote from St John's Gospel enticing you to consider the preferable value of spiritual refreshment.* However, you need to TURN RIGHT out of the car park and follow the lane back to the village's main street. TURN RIGHT here and climb gently up until you reach the Bethesda chapel on your right. BEAR RIGHT here following the sign towards Beaufort. At the end of the houses come to a bridge over the canal. Instead of crossing this, pass through the gap on to the towpath next to a small wharf. TURN LEFT and follow the Brecon and Monmouthshire Canal. *In spring the ground is carpeted by wild flowers such as celandine and violets. The canopy of trees echoes to bird song.* The cut follows a course a little above the valley floor so offering glimpses through the trees across Crickhowell to the Black Mountains.

2 Leave the canal immediately before the third bridge (Pont y Parc). CROSS THE STILE ON YOUR LEFT AND THEN PASS OVER THE BRIDGE to another stile on the far side. TURN LEFT here following the opposite bank of the canal for a few yards to a third stile. Follow the direction of the yellow way marker through a small copse and diagonally across the field beyond, aiming for a barn in the top corner. A stile just to the right of the barn gives access to another field. Follow the left hand side of this for a few yards until a fingerpost marks the point where you can join a tarmac lane via a stile. TURN RIGHT and follow the lane gently up hill. It soon curves right past Wenllan Farm. At a second right hand bend, TURN LEFT, forsaking the lane for a signed 'no through road'. A short stretch of tarmac leads past Ty Mawr. Pass through a gate to the left on to a green lane. *There are good views ahead to the Sugar Loaf and across the Usk Valley to the distinctly shaped Table Mountain above Crickhowell. But you'll have more time to enjoy these later as the lane soon swings right and climbs up the slope. It becomes stonier and can be watery in wet weather. Coppiced hedges are adorned with wild flowers such as foxgloves and herb robert.* You pass a disused chapel on the left at Laswern-Isaf, now a protected site for roosting bats. *The Vincent Wildlife Trust, based in nearby Herefordshire, has established 50 reserves for bats in Wales, England and Ireland.* Just above, some fallen trees have seriously blocked the path, though you can easily avoid these by carefully following the stones around to the right. At the top the lane turns right and levels out. Pass the house at Laswern Fawr and emerge through a gate on to a tarmac track on open mountainside. This track soon leads to a lane.

3 TURN SHARP LEFT and follow the lane a short way until it reaches the entrance to a car park (SO 209154). Follow the access road RIGHT. When it comes to the car park itself, continue ahead past a barrier on to a grassy track climbing gently towards the disused quarries. *The quarries developed because of the canal's construction. Today they are popular with rock climbers and also hide the entrance to an extensive cave system.* A few yards below a ruined kiln, BEAR RIGHT at a junction and follow the track as it contours below the old spoil heaps. After a while the wide track disappears at an area of huge shattered boulders, but a small path weaves its way, SLANTING DOWN TO JOIN A BROAD PATHWAY a little way below.

START

Llangattock

Llangattock Park House

Ty Neuadd

Monmouthshire & Brecon Canal

Pont y Part

Ty Mawr

Wenllan

N

0 Miles

barn

Old chapel

Agen Allwedd

Cwm Onneu Fach

Chwar Mawr

Darren Cilau

When you join this FOLLOW IT LEFT and soon enter the nature reserve of Craig y Cilau. Follow the track, the line of a disused tramway, as it curves around the inner recesses of the cwm. *The residual track offers an almost effortless progress around the mountainside, with dramatic panoramas and intimate views of the cliffs above.*

4 WATCH OUT FOR A SMALL YELLOW MARKER POST on the right. This is your cue to leave the tramway and SLANT DOWN TO THE RIGHT following a smaller path. At another junction, stick with the yellow marker and descend more steeply until you reach a wall at the bottom. TURN SHARP RIGHT here and follow the path through the bracken at the bottom of the valley with a small stream

on your left. Ignore the public footpath sign crossing the stream and climbing into the woods. Now you can see the full majesty of the limestone cliffs ahead of you and the tramway followed earlier. Keep to the path alongside the stream, ignoring alternatives. After a while descend more steeply and roughly until you reach a stile at the bottom of a rough incline.

5 Cross the stile to leave the wooded cwm and enter a field. Keep to the left hand side and soon pick up a green lane. Follow this past a farm, ignoring the access tracks, until a stile leads to a tarmac lane on the right. Cross the stile and follow the lane LEFT back to Llangattock.

TRAINS, TRAMS AND DAMS

DESCRIPTION A 5½-mile exploration of the lower reaches of the Caerfanell valley and its peaceful sylvan subordinate, Cwm Banw. The captivating natural beauty of the woodlands and surrounding hills disguises a wealth of industrial archaeology. Tramway, railroad and reservoir all give clues to the strategic importance of this pass through the mountains. Most of the route has an excellent hard-core surface, making it suitable for a wet day or muddy season.

START Forestry car park, picnic area and campsite between Talybont reservoir and Aber Village. SO 106210.

DIRECTIONS Aber village is situated 2 miles south of Tal-y-bont on the minor road that traverses the mountains towards Merthyr. There is a small roadside parking area if the official car park is closed.

Beacons Bus services operate along this road on summer Sundays and Bank Holidays. Service X43 serves Tal-y-bont (just over a mile north of point 4) from Abergavenny, Brecon, Merthyr and Cardiff. The bus runs every 2 hours on Mondays to Saturdays throughout the year.

1 WALK NORTH along the road, following a footpath sign, 'To the Hill'. Watch for traffic. In about 200 yards, TURN LEFT up a lane with another sign 'To the Hill.' *This refers to Waun Rydd, which rises above the forest to the west. But we're not bound for this apparently definitive elevation.* Just 200 yards up the lane, we leave the route to 'The Hill'. Where the lane bends to the left, look for a stile in the RIGHT HAND fence. CROSS THIS AND CONTINUE ACROSS THE FIELD heading towards an old chapel. *Although the OS map indicates a path below the chapel, there is no access out of the field here.* Instead, a kissing gate leads into the graveyard and a path leads through this on to the lane beyond. TURN LEFT up the lane. This climbs steadily into the hidden wooded recess of Cwm Banw. *Depending on the time of year, enjoy the festival of colour in the*

hedgerow. Bluebells, stichwort, herb robert, cow parsley, garlic mustard and red campion are among the plants that thrive in this habitat. Higher up pass a house and barn. Although the lane is tarmac and open to traffic you are unlikely to encounter motor vehicles; it leads to just one house. A variety of trees provide a sylvan home for bird life. Oak, ash, rowan, silver birch and hawthorn cling to the slope, hiding the stream down below you to the right. A gate leads to more open country. A new section of lane diverts above a landslip. Now you have views ahead of the high ridge from Waun Rydd. To visit this ridge, see **Walk 15**. Eventually the lane ends at Nantllanerch Farm. The homestead sits snugly in the side of the cwm. *The noise of a generator indicates self-sufficiency from the national grid.*

2 At the end of the lane A SERIES OF GATES LEADS ON TO A GREEN TRACK. This is a bridleway and is also a signed mountain bike route. Follow the track down to a ford over a small stream, just above a waterfall. Hug the fence and curve round to the right. After another gate you drop down a shady avenue between two ditches. At the bottom, cross a footbridge over the rocky fast flowing Clydach. The track then climbs up to the right. There are good views back across Cwm Banw; pause to look at the high ridge of Ffordd Las and Waun Rydd behind you. After a while, the lane gains a surface and continues through pine forest. *As you emerge from the trees, there are views of Tal-y-bont reservoir and east to the Black Mountains.*

3 TURN RIGHT over a stile, following a sign for Aber. You have now joined the Usk Valley Walk. Follow the left hand side of the field above the house at Pwll-y-hwyaid and find a stile under a tree just to the left of a gate. Cross the next field to another stile and descend the subsequent field diagonally. At the bottom, a post indicates the way to a short section of green lane leading to the road.

4 TURN RIGHT along the road, watching for traffic. In about 300 yards, opposite

Aber Farm, TURN LEFT through a gate, still following the Usk Valley Walk. Follow the left hand side of the field, through another gate and on to a footbridge. At the far side, ignore the path to the right and continue STRAIGHT AHEAD, across a grassy strip, and then up through a patch of woodland.

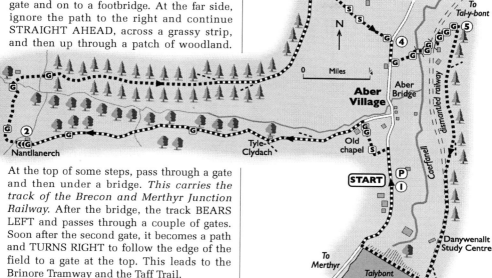

At the top of some steps, pass through a gate and then under a bridge. *This carries the track of the Brecon and Merthyr Junction Railway.* After the bridge, the track BEARS LEFT and passes through a couple of gates. Soon after the second gate, it becomes a path and TURNS RIGHT to follow the edge of the field to a gate at the top. This leads to the Brinore Tramway and the Taff Trail.

5 TURN RIGHT to follow the line of the old Tramroad. At an intersection of tracks, BEAR RIGHT and descend gently, leaving the Tramroad to ascend through the woods. After a while join the track bed of the Brecon and Merthyr Junction Railway and follow this to Tal-y-bont reservoir. TURN RIGHT to cross the dam wall. At the end of the dam, TURN RIGHT and follow the road carefully back to the start.

Brinore Tramroad

The Tramroad opened in 1815, the year of the Battle of Waterloo. It was built to carry limestone from the quarries at Trefil, and coal from mines near Tredegar. The minerals were carried across the mountains to the canal wharf at Tal-y-bont. Horses pulled the trams up hill, while they freewheeled back down, using a wooden wedge to jam the wheels if gravity proved too generous. The tramway declined with the rise of the railways in the second half of the nineteenth century. For more details, look at the Brinore Tramroad Conservation Forum (http://brinore-tramroad.powys.org.uk/forum.htm).

Brecon and Merthyr Junction Railway

In 1858, an Act of Parliament allowed the construction of the Brecon and Merthyr Junction Railway. It eventually ran a network of lines between Newport and Brecon, providing a link between one of the world's foremost ports and mid Wales. Between Pant and Tal-y-bont, it passed through the mountains and included the 666-yard long Torpantau tunnel. The main section was closed to passenger traffic in 1962, but the route through the Beacons now forms part of the Taff Trail, a 58-mile cycling and walking route from Brecon to Cardiff. Part of the track has been reopened as the Brecon Mountain Railway (see **Walk 10**).

Tal-y-bont Reservoir

This was built to quench Newport's thirst in the 1930s. More recently, Talybont-on-Usk Energy, a community group, took over the disused turbine house to generate hydro electricity, which is sold to the national grid.

LLANGYNIDR, TOR Y FOEL & THE CANAL

DESCRIPTION A 7½ mile walk with an excellent variety of Beacons scenery. You sample the uplands through climbing the grassy 551m pyramid of Tor y Foel, but the climb is not as long or strenuous as the highest peaks. The summit is a good viewpoint over the Usk and Caerfanell valleys. The return route descends through fields to the Brecon and Monmouthshire Canal. This gives a gentle and pleasant walk back to Llangynidr.

START Car Park, opposite Llangynidr village hall. SO 156196.

DIRECTIONS The village of Llangynidr lies on the southern side of the river Usk between Crickhowell and Brecon. The B4558 runs through the village. The direct road from Llangynidr to the A40 at Bwlch crosses the river on a very narrow bridge, only suitable for ordinary cars. Otherwise, access the village via Crickhowell or Tal-y-bont. The car park is on the B4558 on the eastern side of the village. There are toilets opposite.

Bus X43 runs from Abergavenny to Brecon and Merthyr via Llangynidr village. It stops outside the car park.

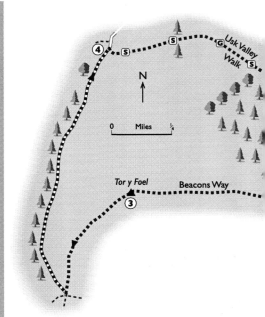

1 Walk WEST towards the main village for a few yards. Just opposite an old chapel, now a cycle manufacturer, TURN RIGHT across a stile. Walk down the left hand side of the field. At the end, take a few steps left to find another stile. Cross this and continue across the fields to the canal. Cross the bridge and follow the towpath LEFT along the canal. A lovely tree lined stretch offers views across to Bwlch on the other side of the Usk valley. The canal bypasses the village and arrives at the Lower Lock at the bottom of the Llangynidr flight. *The Coach and Horses lies just to the left, but perhaps it's too early for refreshment!* Just after a winding hole (a wider turning point on the canal) you come to Depot Lock (No 65).

2 A footpath crosses the canal just in front of the lock. CROSS THIS and follow the footpath signposted with The Beacons Way logo. Follow the path through some beech and oak woods with the Afon Crawnon tumbling down to your left. Emerging from the woods, you can see our goal, Tor y Foel, rising up to the right. Follow the waymarks up the fields, crossing a number of stiles and a farm access road. At the top of the fields, the path comes out on to an access road by a couple of houses at Pen-y-beili. At the end of this access road, go STRAIGHT ACROSS the road and continue up a bridleway opposite. After a while this green lane comes up to open hillside. Keep climbing steadily and inexorably towards the top, being prepared for a few false summits! Although steep in places, the way is grassy and springy underfoot and there are excellent views on both sides of the long ridge.

3 At 551 metres, Tor y Foel is by no means the highest ground in the area. But, because it stands alone, there are great all-round views. The ground drops away beyond the summit into the Caerfanell valley and Tal-y-bont reservoir. From the summit BEAR

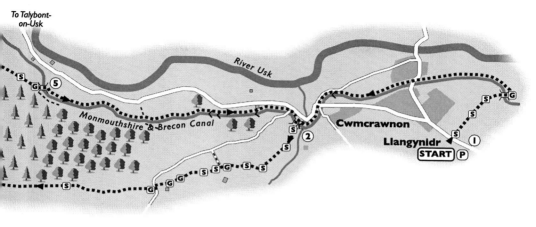

LEFT to continue on the broad and obvious track south westwards. It descends to the end of a tarmac road at a bwlch. Turn sharp right to follow this very quiet mountain road with a lovely panorama of Tal-y-bont reservoir and the forest below you.

4 After about a mile, and just before a cattle grid, TURN RIGHT at a footpath sign. *This is now the Usk Valley Walk.* Follow the track as it curves round to a gate and a stile (don't follow another track up hill). Follow the path gently down across the field, through a small strip of conifers and across the next field, gradually dropping to the fence. Find a gate in the bottom left hand corner. Continue to follow the way markers across the fields and through a patch of woodland until you reach the canal.

5 CROSS THE CANAL and go down the steps to join the towpath. Follow this eastward and enjoy the wild flowers and trees. You pass the Llangynidr flight of locks and after a while, rejoin the outward route at lock **65**. Continue back on your outward route, or if you prefer, leave the canal to walk through the village.

Monmouthshire & Brecon Canal

The navigation opened in 1812, connecting Brecon with Newport. It played a key role in the transport of minerals from the Monmouthshire iron and coalfields to the greatest port in the world. Stone from the great quarries of Llangattock and Trefil was brought by tramway to the canal and transported onwards by barge. By the 1930s the cut had fallen into disuse. But in 1970 British Waterways Board reopened parts and a 32-mile stretch from Brecon to Pontypool is now accessible for navigation. It is a very pleasant route.

River Usk

The river rises in south west of Sennybridge and travels through Brecon, Abergavenny and Usk to meet the Severn estuary at Newport. Its lower reaches are very deep and also have a very high tidal range, up to 30 feet. These features enabled the growth of Newport as one of the world's major ports in the nineteenth century. Its upper reaches, west of Brecon, forms a key route from western Wales into England and its fertile valley forms some of the richest farming land in the country. A narrow sixteenth century bridge spans the river near Llangynidr, still open to light traffic.

A CIRCUIT OF PONTSTICILL RESERVOIR

DESCRIPTION There is a range of scenery on this 6-mile circuit of Pontsticill reservoir, the largest of four reservoirs in the Taf Fechan valley. On the east side, you traverse some high-level moor land and limestone pasture, while the western half of the walk makes use of the Taff Trail as it weaves its way through mixed woodland en route for Brecon. Views of the reservoir dominate much of the journey and there is an eye-catching panorama of Pen y Fan rising on the northern skyline above the Taf Fechan Forest. You also make the close acquaintance of the Brecon Mountain Railway.

START Car Park near Dolygaer, at the head of the reservoir. SO 144054.

DIRECTIONS Leave the A470 or A465 at Cefn-coed-y-cymmer, just north of Merthyr. Follow signs to Pontsticill and continue through the village towards Tal-y-bont. Pass along the west side of Pontsticill Reservoir. Just before the end, where the road turns left, continue ahead on a cul-de-sac. The car park is just on your left. You can also approach from Tal-y-bont in the north.

Beacons Bus serves the road junction near the starting point and Pontsticill village on Sundays and Bank Holidays during summer. Stagecoach bus 24 runs between Merthyr bus station and Pontsticill village around every 2 hours Monday to Saturdays. You could leave the bus at the Red Cow and start from point 5.

1 TURN LEFT out of the car park and follow the road as it crosses the bridge between Pontsticill and Pentwyn reservoirs with fine views both ways. Continue along the road until it comes to a railway bridge. Just before the road goes underneath this, TURN RIGHT to follow a path descending steeply down to the lakeshore. After a brief encounter with the water's edge, it climbs back up through the woods to run alongside the track of the Brecon Mountain Railway.

Steam trains run between Pant station and this point, before returning to Pontsticill station on the return journey. The path widens into a track just above the sailing club.

2 Just past the club you come to a yellow-topped post, opposite a bridge under the railway. TURN LEFT under the bridge following a bridleway sign. At this point the main track continues level along the side of the reservoir to Pontsticill station. It is not an official right of way but seems to be used with constant impunity by tourists and locals alike as a convenient stroll and dog walk, as well as being vehicular access to the sailing club. However, our official route follows a bridleway up the hill. *It has the advantage of spectacular views across the reservoir and a sense of superiority over the mortals down below.* The route climbs steeply and diagonally up the hillside through woodland, gaining views across the reservoir. At the top of the woods, come to a gate giving access to the open moorland. Go through this. The bridleway now becomes indistinct and irrelevant. The key to the next section is the forest on your right. FOLLOW THE EDGE OF THIS, 100 YARDS OR SO ABOVE IT. A faint path appears but soon disappears in a rather marshy area. But the dampness is soon over. Maintain your line, with the forest edge as your guide, until you come to a small ravine just above a confluence of two streams. Climb carefully down the rather loose sheep path to the stream and continue along a narrow track on the other side. This brings you to a bridge made from an old railway sleeper that crosses the second stream.

3 Continue in the direction indicated by the plank, climbing gently up the slope in the direction of some fence posts on the horizon. If this sounds rather complicated, it is less so on the ground. Remember, the edge of the forest is the key – you are skirting just above the boundary of this on open access land. As you reach the fence continue ahead with the wall bedside you. Great views open out. You have just crossed a geological boundary and are now walking on limestone. It's much easier going and well drained. *Be careful not to follow the fence* as it drops precipitously down the edge of a disused lime-

18

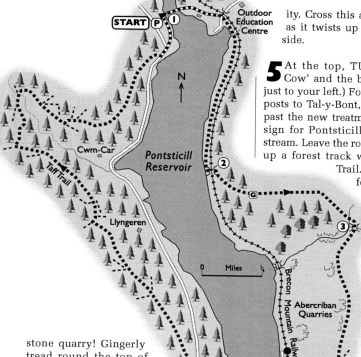

ity. Cross this and follow the side road as it twists up the hill on the opposite side.

5 At the top, TURN RIGHT ('The Red Cow' and the bus stop for Merthyr are just to your left.) Follow the road, with signposts to Tal-y-Bont, through the village and past the new treatment works. Just past the sign for Pontsticill reservoir, you cross a stream. Leave the road here and TURN LEFT up a forest track with a sign for the Taff Trail. It rises gently into the forest. Later it narrows to a tarmac footpath to cross a ravine on a wooden footbridge. *This is a lovely spot on the edge of the forest, with a convenient seat.* At a junction of paths, BEAR LEFT keeping on the Taff Trail. Where it returns to the road, TURN LEFT. Soon keep straight on at a junction to follow the 'no through road' back to the car park.

stone quarry! Gingerly tread round the top of the unguarded cliff and notice the pitons used for rock climbing. You pick up a faint path just a little way from the edge of the escarpment. Just after a wood on your right, you come to a metal gate with a blue-topped lever. There is also a wooden post a few yards above. This gate marks re-entry to enclosed land.

4 TURN RIGHT through it and follow the regained bridleway dropping down diagonally above the reservoir dam, with the brooding heights of the Beacons presiding over the northern horizon. Pass under the Brecon Mountain Railway, across an access track, and on down the lane to the road at the bottom. Go through the gate into the road. TURN LEFT AND THEN IMMEDIATELY RIGHT, past Pontsticill Water Treatment works to reach the bridge over the river, admiring the vaguely ecclesiastical architecture of the ex-municipal util-

Brecon Mountain Railway

Steam trains operate from Easter to November, with some additional Christmas specials at the end of the year. The preserved railway has operated since 1980. For much of the way, including this section, it runs along the course of the Brecon and Merthyr Railway. The first train ran on 8th August 1868 and over the years the railway brought many visitors into the Beacons and carried farmers' products from the hills to the towns. In 1873, the local rector counted 21 trains in one day – he must have had a busy life! The line closed in 1964. The current reopened route runs from Pant station, above Merthyr, past limestone quarries and along the length of Pontsticill reservoir. For details, see:
www.breconmountainrailway.co.uk

GLYNTAWE AND PENWYLLT

DESCRIPTION This walk is short in distance, but rich in historical and geological interest. During the course of 4 miles you encounter the remains of one of the highest railways in Wales, while under your feet lies the deepest cave system in the country. In between, the infant River Tawe forges a path through spectacular limestone crags and the attractive arbour of Craig-y-nos Country Park.

START Craig-y-nos Country Park. SN 840155.

DIRECTIONS Craig-y-nos lies aside the A4067 Swansea – Brecon road in the upper Swansea valley, just south of Glyntawe. There is a National Park Visitor Centre here. The car park charge contributes to the National Park's work of conservation and recreation, so pay it with a good heart! A plethora of local attractions include the Dan-yr-ogof show caves and the Shire Horse Centre, as well as the country park itself.

Beacons Bus services stop outside the park on summer Sundays and Bank Holidays. Stagecoach bus 63 (Swansea-Brecon) also calls here three times a day (no Sunday service).

1 Start outside the visitor centre and go down the steps in front of you. Follow the path through a brick gateway, past the fishpond and down to the river. TURN RIGHT, passing a confluence of rivers and then TURN LEFT to cross the Afon Tawe by a footbridge. On the far side TURN LEFT to follow the Tawe upstream.

2 In about a quarter of a mile, some stepping-stones lead across the river. This would be an unwise choice as a misplaced stone in the middle makes it a risky enterprise. Instead, CROSS THE FOOTBRIDGE and go through a gate. Cross a small but rather soggy wood to another gate. Beyond this follow the way marks through a marshy area, helped by duckboards. Cross a stile to reach the main road. CROSS THE ROAD CAREFULLY, to a stile on the opposite side. Follow the path between two fields and

climb slightly to reach a car park. TURN RIGHT through the car park. *As you are about to pass the wide car park access road, notice a reconstructed dolmen on your right, interpreting a prehistoric burial site. The stone circles only date from the year 2000, erected to celebrate the present millennium!* KEEP STRAIGHT ON past the access road, towards the campsite. On your right is the Shire Horse Centre. The field is also home to other animals including goats, sheep and llamas.

3 At the end of the animal field, TURN LEFT following a finger post off the road. The path now climbs left above the campsite. After a kissing gate, pass a sheepfold and keep straight ahead as the path descends to the rocky bed of the Afon Haffes. CROSS THE WATER at a convenient place, making use of the stones. This is not especially hazardous in normal conditions, but care is needed on the rocks and especially if they are slippery or the river is in spate. On the opposite bank, look for a gate and stile in the fence. FOLLOW THE PATH AND LANE DOWN through a series of gates and past a restored house until you reach the main road.

4 WALK OVER THE ROAD carefully and TURN LEFT along it for a short distance, crossing the River Tawe. Opposite a phone box, TURN RIGHT along Heol Callwen. Continue along the road past the houses and on to Pwllcoediog Farm. In the farmyard, TURN LEFT following a public footpath sign. Climb diagonally up the hillside crossing a series of stiles. After a patch of woodland you soon emerge at the top. *A completely different landscape lies ahead of you. The bustle of the valley is left behind. In front lies a lunar terrain of limestone crags, pockmarked by quarries and loose rocks.* Follow the path as it weaves a way past a disused quarry and emerges on to a lane. You have now reached the old quarrying village of Penwyllt. TURN LEFT and follow the lane a short way to its terminus.

5 In front of view are the remains of Penwyllt railway station, complete with platforms and station buildings. Beyond lies

Penwyllt quarry, still working today. TURN RIGHT past the station and follow the stony road round the perimeter of the quarry. This ends at a row of old quarry houses, now a caving centre. *Just before this a footpath sign indicates the cross-country route to the Nedd Fechan valley. A bleak but atmospheric cross country route now followed by The Beacons Way leads east to join Sarn Helen, the old Roman road, about 3½ miles to the south east (joining* **Walk 14** *just before point* **3**). In front of the terrace, TURN RIGHT and follow the path through a kissing gate and across the track of the old railway. Negotiate the accompanying ditch, cross a stile and follow the path up to a ruined building, noting remains of lime kilns to the left. Just in front of the house TURN RIGHT and follow the track across the rough pasture. It returns to the top of the road, just near the station at point **5**. TURN LEFT and follow the road downhill.

6 About 100 yards after a bungalow on your right, where the road begins to veer to the left, GO THROUGH A GATE ON THE RIGHT HAND SIDE, indicated by a bridle way sign. Descend the rhiw amidst bracken and flowers. Towards the bottom it becomes more wooded and stony. At the end, go through a gate and TURN RIGHT on to the tarmac lane. Follow this a few yards to its end in front of Rhongyr-uchaf farm. A gate just to the left of the house gives access to a walled lane through the woods. In just over half a mile, TURN LEFT through a gate in the fence on your left. Follow the path for a few yards back to point 2 by the stepping-stones. TURN LEFT and retrace your steps back to the visitor centre.

Craig-y-nos Country Park

Craig-y-nos first developed as an estate in the mid nineteenth century. The house was used as a hospital between 1919 and 1980, but in 1976 the Brecon Beacons National Park Authority turned the grounds into a country park. There are woods, riverside walks and meadows to enjoy and a visitor centre interprets the landscape.

Dan-yr-ogof

You can explore part of the vast labyrinth of limestone caverns at Dan-yr-ogof, where the River Llynell emerges from the rock. Among other attractions on the site are a Shire Horse Centre, a dinosaur park, and a reconstruction of a 100-year old farm. (Entrance charge).

Penwyllt

High on a shelf above the Tawe valley, Penwyllt developed as a centre for limestone quarrying and the production of lime. Silica sand was also extracted nearby. Between 1867 and 1962 passenger trains ran between Neath and Brecon. The station at Penwyllt, still broadly intact, was paid for by Adelina Platt, the opera singer, who lived at Craig-y-nos. Ogof Ffynnon Ddu Nature reserve extends from Penwyllt across a large area of limestone crag and pavement beyond. The name translates as cave of the black spring, the deepest cave system in Britain.

PONT MELIN FACH AND WATERFALL COUNTRY

DESCRIPTION The Mellte, Hepste and Nedd Fechan all drain the wild limestone uplands in the southern part of the national park. As they travel south, they cross belts of harder sandstone rock, which the water has eroded less than the neighbouring shale. Here is where the waterfalls are formed. This is a popular area of the national park, often referred to as 'Waterfall Country'. There is a range of walks for all abilities. Paths pass through wooded gorges where fast flowing streams tumble down spectacular waterfalls on their way from the mountains to the sea. **Walks 12, 13** and **14** provide three possibilities for exploring the region. This 6-mile circuit starts by following the Nedd Fechan from Pontneddfechan to Pont Melin Fach known as the 'Elidir Trail'. The fast flowing river travels down a series of falls, viewed from the path. After Pont Melin Fach, a quiet lane climbs to common land at Comin y Rhos, with extensive views across the forest away to the sea beyond. A woodland track descends to the opposite bank of the Nedd Fechan for the final leg. Shorter linear alternatives are described below.

START The Tourist Information Centre, opposite the Angel Hotel, Pontneddfechan. SN 902076

DIRECTIONS The village of Pontneddfechan lies close to the A465 Hirwaun-Neath road. Leave this main road at Glyn-neath and follow the signs. The walk starts in the centre of the village by the Angel Hotel and opposite the Tourist Information Centre. There is a small car park and some roadside parking here.

There is a limited bus service on Route 161 from Neath and Swansea (not Sundays). Beacons Bus serves Pontneddfechan on summer Sundays and bank holidays.

1 The path begins opposite the Tourist Information Centre in Pontneddfechan. Pass through the iron gates marked 'Sgwd Gwladus'. Follow the path, which is suitable for pushchairs and wheelchairs for the first mile. *It follows the line of an old tramway and the stone sets are still visible in places. Mixed deciduous woodland, including sycamore, beech and oak trees, provide habitats for a variety of woodland birds. You may see grey wagtails or dippers in the river itself. There are some cave entrances in the rocks on the left. A picnic area marks the limit of navigation for pushchairs and wheelchairs.* The path continues up some steps and onwards to the confluence of the Nedd Fechan and Pyrddin at Pwll Du ar Byrddin.

2 From here you can visit Sgwd Gwladus by KEEPING LEFT and following the path to the pretty waterfall. Return to the junction at point **2**. Then CROSS THE FOOTBRIDGE and pass a finger post. Keep to the LEFT HAND bank of the Nedd Fechan, ignoring the second footbridge and following the sign to Pont Melin Fach. The path clings to the side of the river, passing a series of waterfalls. *Ravines cut into the cliffs, gouged out by water cascading down into the river below.* The gorge opens out at the picnic area and car park at Pont Melin Fach.

3 TURN RIGHT and cross the road bridge. Follow the quiet lane as it twists uphill to the common at Comin y Rhos. *Magnificent views are your reward. The slightly raised ground offers unimpeded vistas of a wide segment of southern Wales. If the air is clear, look southwest to see the rocks of Mumbles reaching out into Swansea Bay.* Carry on past the crossroads on the top of the common. Where the open land ends, TURN RIGHT across a cattle grid to follow the access road towards Gwernblaedde Farm. Continue past the farm and the water treatment works until the road becomes a forest track. This ends by a house at Glan-yr-afon. FOLLOW THE PATH LEFT from here. It descends through woodland to meet the river at the bottom.

4 TURN LEFT to follow the riverside path signed for Pontneddfechan. In places it is narrow and requires some care. At a finger post it DOUBLES BACK and zigzags up the hill away from the river. At the top cross a stile and follow the path with the fence on your right through light woodland. Cross a footbridge guarded by two stiles. At the far side choose the left hand of two stiles and make your way through a short section of soggy woodland, past a school and on to the road. You are now in Pontneddfechan. TURN RIGHT down the road between the houses. At a bend, by a bus shelter, follow a lane straight ahead. This drops

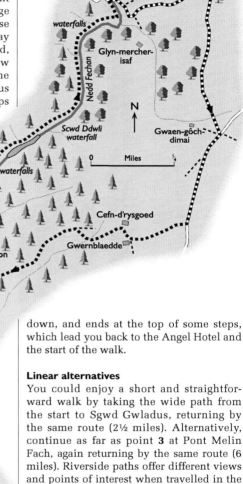

Glyn-mercher-uchaf

waterfalls

Glyn-mercher-isaf

Nedd Fechan

N

Scwd Ddwli waterfall

Gwaen-gôch-dimai

0   Miles   ¼

waterfalls

Cefn-d'rysgoed

waterfall

Gwernblaedde

Sgwd Gwladus waterfall

Glan-yr-afon

down, and ends at the top of some steps, which lead you back to the Angel Hotel and the start of the walk.

Linear alternatives

You could enjoy a short and straightforward walk by taking the wide path from the start to Sgwd Gwladus, returning by the same route (2½ miles). Alternatively, continue as far as point **3** at Pont Melin Fach, again returning by the same route (6 miles). Riverside paths offer different views and points of interest when travelled in the opposite direction.

Pontneddfechan

START   B4242

WALK 13
PENDERYN AND SGWD YR EIRA

DESCRIPTION An interesting circuit of woods and uplands at the southern end of 'Waterfall Country'. The outward section of this 5½ mile walk climbs through attractive heath and moor to the village of Penderyn, home of Wales' whiskey industry. The return follows a wooded ridge high above the gorge carved by the Afon Mellte on its way through the limestone bedrock. The noise of birdsong and waterfalls accompany you much of the way. The route can be muddy between points **2** and **3**. Please note the comments below about Sgwd yr Eira.

START Forestry Commission car park at Dinas Rock, Pontneddfechan. SN 911079.

DIRECTIONS Pontneddfechan sits astride the confluence of the Nedd Fechan and Mellte rivers at the foot of 'Waterfall Country'. To reach the village, leave the A465 Hirwaun-Neath road at Glyn-neath and follow the signs. To find the start of **Walk 13** continue past the information centre for another half mile until you reach the end of the road and the Dinas Rock car park. Note that the car park is locked after dark.

There is a limited bus service on Route 161 from Neath and Swansea to Pontneddfechan (not Sundays). You could also start this walk from Penderyn. There is a half-hourly bus service to here from Aberdare (Route 7), with a more limited service on Sundays (Route 6). There are also three buses each weekday between Penderyn and Brecon (Route 742). Beacons Bus serves Pontneddfechan and Penderyn on summer Sundays and bank holidays.

I Climb the stony track just to the north of the car park, signposted to the waterfalls. This rises up the side of the rock, Craig-y-ddinas, and on through the woods. It climbs along a narrow neck of limestone rock between the afon Mellte and a small tributary. *Quarrying has eaten into the bedrock, but the crag is capped by delightful limestone heathland with soft, springy turf.* At the top of the heath, KEEP TO THE RIGHT

alongside the fence. The path passes through an area of old quarries and rises up through the bracken. There is now a long, but steady ascent on a charming bridleway. *The views widen. Beyond a gate you enter wilder country. In the distance on the right, you can see Tower Colliery, Wales' last deep coal mine.* After the summit the track descends gently towards Penderyn. It joins a small tarmac lane through a gate. Follow this ahead as it winds around St Cynog's church. *This has been a Christian place of worship since the sixth century and the graveyard is now maintained as a wildlife haven.* The lane drops down to skirt the village of Penderyn. Unless visiting the village continue straight ahead until the last houses. A diversion to the right will bring you to the main road, a pub and a bus stop. *Not far from here is Wales' only distillery, making Penderyn whiskey in a modest and easily mistakable shed alongside the main road. Penderyn makes a convenient alternative start to this walk if you're travelling by bus from Aberdare or Brecon. If you start from here join the route by walking up the road by the Lamb Hotel and turn right at the end to the last houses and Point 2.*

2 TURN LEFT along a track in front of a couple of cottages. A footpath sign set a little way back indicates the route to Sgwd yr Eira. At the end of the lane a gate leads into open access land. The track follows the course of an old tramway and soon comes to some old quarries. Keep beside the fence on your right and follow the guide marks, crossing an area of damp rough pasture towards some trees. CROSS THE STILE AND BEAR LEFT up the side of the plantation. Soon the ground drops away towards the Hepste valley. The path goes through some soggy areas but the line is clear.

3 Arrive at a finger post pointing the way down to Sgwd yr Eira whose Welsh name means 'waterfall of the snow'. *You can*

24

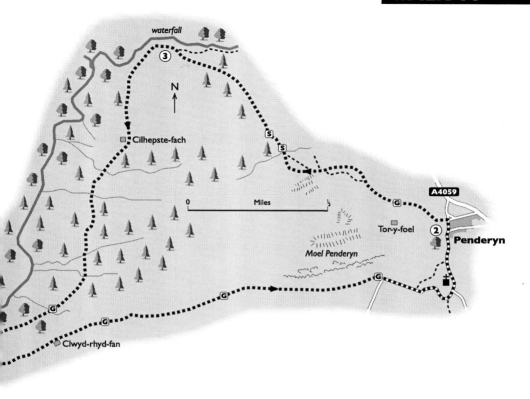

hear the noise as a curtain of water plunges down a rocky cliff amidst dense woodland. However, in 2007 the path to the waterfall from here was closed for safety reasons. Until the path is re-opened you should not venture down to the fall itself. Even before its closure it was a steep and difficult path and the rocks at the bottom were very slippery. For up to date information, visit www.brecon-beacons.org. At the fingerpost, take the path towards Craig-y-ddinas. The path now follows the top of the limestone gorge. *Soon there are picturesque views across the forest, with the confluence of Pyrddin and Nedd Fechan rivers hidden in the trees below. Later you can see the Neath valley snaking its way towards Swansea.* Continue on this path as it

returns to the limestone heath and quarries at Craig-y-ddinas and descends to the car park and starting point.

Craig-y-ddinas

A legend claims that Craig-y-ddinas is the rock under which King Arthur sleeps, waiting to rescue Wales from the Saxon invaders. A tale relates how a Welshman from London visited a cavern under the rock and found the king, with his knights, asleep inside. He was told he could take the gold and silver from the slumbering heroes, but had to remember to tell them to 'sleep on'. On the first occasion he remembered, but predictably forgot on his second trip. His greed was met with destruction.

25

YSTRADFELLTE, SARN HELEN AND LIMESTONE COUNTRY

DESCRIPTION An exhilarating 8-mile expedition into the wild uplands around the head of the Nedd Fechan. The route crosses limestone pastures, broken by rocky crags and dotted with limekilns. It follows the line of Sarn Helen, the Roman road from Neath to Brecon, for several miles through forest and moorland. There is real variety of scenery and, above all, a sense of space and freedom. Although the walk does not climb to the highest peaks, it is a long trail, crossing some remote and lonely country, so go well prepared. Some sections require careful navigation. A shorter alternative is also given.

START Ystradfellte village car park. SN 930134.

DIRECTIONS Ystradfellte is accessed by a minor road, which crosses the mountains between Pontneddfechan (see **walks 12** and **13**) and Sennybridge (on the A40 Brecon-Llandovery road).

There is no public transport near this route.

I Take the narrow lane up the hill by the side of the car park. Where the tarmac ends, carry STRAIGHT ON up a sunken green lane. At the top a gate leads into open country. *The track keeps ascending gently though limestone pasture, dotted with rocks and occasional hawthorn trees. Higher up another gate carries the track into an area of shattered limestone crags. You pass a few ponds and, on your right, a restored lime kiln, offering evidence of the industrial importance of this area in times past.* Just past the kiln, cross a stile and join a green lane. *Ahead the rounded tops of Fan Nedd and Fan Llia rise above the wild moors and forest.* In about ½ mile the lane comes to a road. This is the pass over to Sennybridge. Follow the road LEFT and ascend gently through moors and trees. You pass a Forestry Commission car park on the right at Blaen Llia.

2 A few hundred yards further, TURN SHARP LEFT through a gate on to a stony track, signposted 'Sarn Helen', a cross-mountain Roman road between forts near Brecon and at Neath. *You have now also joined the route of the Beacons Way. You soon pass through the site of a Roman Camp. This is an atmospheric traverse of wild and lonely country, all the more so on a grey or misty day, when you can imagine the legions of soldiers or farmers crossing these uplands. Just after a second gate you pass a solitary standing stone, Maen Madoc.* Continue through remote upland country, now dropping to the Nedd Fechan. Cross the river using a new wooden footbridge that replaces the risky ford. FOLLOW THE TRACK UP THE OPPOSITE BANK with the buildings of Blaen Nedd Fechan below you to the left. At the top of the hill, go through a gate to a junction of paths. Leave the Beacons Way here, instead TURNING LEFT to stay on Sarn Helen. *The Beacons Way crosses desolate limestone moor to reach Penwyllt, above the upper Swansea valley, in about 3½ miles. It joins* **Walk 11** *near point* **5**. Our route and the line of the Roman road continue beside a wood to another gate. In another 50 yards, come to a junction of paths.

3 *A shorter alternative route leaves to the left here (see below).* Otherwise, CONTINUE AHEAD on Sarn Helen. The track finds a terrace on the hillside, the valley of the Nedd Fechan below and limestone scars and forest to the right. It continues through rough and boggy pasture grazed by cattle. At a depression, the route SWINGS UP TO THE RIGHT in front of some forest and rises gently with trees on the left and moor on the right.

4 At a gate and stile TURN LEFT and follow a good track into the forest. This is a bridleway and drops gradually through the forest. After about a mile, BEAR LEFT at a junction. Almost immediately, just a few yards on, watch carefully for a rather muddy but clear four-wheel track diving down into the undergrowth to the right. TURN RIGHT and follow it. It's not as bad as it looks, and is, in fact, the continuation of the bridleway. But it could easily be missed.

The track is wet and muddy at the top but soon improves. A rocky section leads down to the Nedd Fechan, which is crossed by a bridge. Climb steeply up the opposite bank on a stony track. It emerges from the woods and reaches a road.

5 TURN RIGHT. In a few yards TURN LEFT at a junction. Almost immediately, BEAR RIGHT through a gate along a bridleway signed to Porth yr Ogof. A short way along here, be careful to follow the bridleway markers LEFT, rather than staying on the access track. Continue on down the bridleway. It gets drier as it enters limestone country. Just above a pothole, you come to a road at Cwm Porth.

6 CROSS THE ROAD AND GO THROUGH THE CAR PARK. *There are toilets and an information centre here. From the car park, a side path leads left down the bank to the cave entrance at Porth yr Ogof. The Afon Mellte disappears underground here to emerge 250 yards downstream. The water has sculpted over a mile of caves in the limestone. Walking trails lead from this point to the waterfalls further down the Afon Mellte. At the far end of the car park, GO THROUGH A GATE on to a footpath signed to Ystradfellte. Follow this through the woods and above the farm at Porth yr Ogof. At the road, TURN LEFT and follow it back down into Ystradfellte.*

Alternative shorter route from Point 3.
At the junction, TURN LEFT on to another track. This is a delightful descent through hawthorn trees to the river. Cross the bridge and continue up the other side to meet the road. TURN LEFT. In about 200 yards, TURN RIGHT through a gate following the bridleway sign to Ystradfellte. Cross a small field and then on up through a patch of young

rowan trees. A gate at the top leads to open heath. Continue across this limestone country through series of gates. Just over

Maen Madoc
Sarn Helen
Roman Road

Coed-y-Garreg
kiln
Blaen-nedd-isaf
Blaen Llia
short route
Ystradfellte
Tyle
START
N
Nedd Fechan
Afon Mellte
0 Miles ½

the brow of the hill, go through a final gate to a big expanse of open land. There is no obvious route on the ground from here, but the bridleway just crosses the rough pasture in the direction indicated by the marker. You are aiming for a gate in the far corner of the enclosure, though you can't see it yet. Cross a track in a depression in the middle of the rough ground. Continue on to reach the gate, rejoining the outward route. Pass through this and follow the track back down to Ystradfellte.

A CIRCUIT OF CWM OERGWM

DESCRIPTION An excellent route to the highest ground of the Beacons. The lower slopes provide an idyllic and intimate approach to the mountains. A waterside path with mature trees frames the distinctive sandstone caps of the Beacons. The climb up to the ridge is long but well graded. Once the height is gained, you have a day of airy and straightforward ridge walking with great all-round views. At over 10 miles, this is a long expedition and much of it is at exposed, high altitude. So take careful mountain precautions and avoid it in poor visibility.

START Llanfrynach village. SO 075257. There is no car park, but it is easy to park sensibly on the roadside in the village.

DIRECTIONS Llanfrynach is three miles south east of Brecon, just off the A40 to Abergavenny. Leave the A40 half a mile east of the end of the Brecon by-pass. Turn south down the B4538 towards Tal-y-bont, immediately crossing the canal and Usk. A quarter of mile further, turn off south to follow a minor road to Llanfrynach village.

Bus X43 Abergavenny – Brecon – Merthyr – Cardiff passes through Llanfrynach every 2 hours (no Sunday service).

1 Next to the village hall, TURN UP THE SIDE ROAD signed to 'Cantref'. Just past Tyfry farm, the lane bears to the right. At this point, GO THROUGH THE KISSING GATE ahead of you on to the bridleway. Pass through a field of mature trees with the imposing house of Maesderwen to the right and the Nant Menasgin to your left. The track is obvious and the gentle pastoral scene is a delightful start to a walk with wilder pleasures in store. When the bridleway parts company with the stream, follow the way marks gently up hill to Tynllwyn farm. Passing the farm, take the path through the gate signed to 'the Hill'. Keep to the right hand side of the next field. Our first objective, Cefn Cyff ridge, rises up ahead, while the higher ground of the Beacons looms beyond. Maintain your direction, crossing a

small lane and then emerging on to a narrow road. TURN LEFT and follow this between hedges past a couple of houses until the tarmac ends. TURN RIGHT following the stony track signed to Fan y Big. A short way further on a gate gives access to the open hillside.

2 A clear path climbs quite steeply up the ridge, but offers good views across the valleys on either side. After a steady ascent, the ridge levels out. *This is skylark country. This bird has suffered decline in recent years, but it still seems abundant in the Beacons. Its continuous shrill song haunts the air of these hills. The notched summit of Fan y Big comes into view, while to the right the steep ridge of Bryn Teg leads to the summit of Cribyn. A glance at its merciless gradient makes you grateful that particular route has unaccountably been omitted from this book. Beyond the summit of Cribyn, the sloping plateau of Pen y Fan crowns the highest ground in the Beacons.* As the ridge steepens once again, enjoy close views of the head of the cwm, with the Roman road crossing the 'Gap', the high pass of Bwlch ar y Fan. A narrower, more airy stretch leads directly to the summit of Fan y Big.

3 *It is immediately evident that Fan y Big's status as a major peak is due to its position at the head of the rocky spur you have just climbed. Beyond it the ground climbs gently round the summit ridge. But take care! There is a precipitous drop to the northwest.* The route now lies STRAIGHT AHEAD, almost exactly due south. Take a bearing in mist (180°). The path is clear and a stone windbreak soon confirms your course is correct. The track continues on the edge of the summit ridge with very gentle gradients. *To the right views open out across the Neuadd reservoirs with the headwaters of the Taf Fechan.* Some slate spoil marks the col at Craig Cwmoergwm and the direct path from 'the Gap' joins from the right. BEAR LEFT to join the stone setts climbing the next section. At the top the path VEERS LEFT to a north-north easterly direction, still hugging the edge of the escarpment. *The successive ridges of the central Beacons range westwards, presided over by Pen y Fan, supported by its buttress, Corn Du. Together they seem to* *crouch over the Usk valley like a pair of lions guarding their territory.* The edge and the path suddenly TURN SHARP RIGHT and you reach the highest point of the walk at Bwlch y Ddwyallt (754m), though you would hardly notice, as there is no dramatic topographical feature to underline its significance. Keep following the path, which becomes grassier and begins to descend towards the Usk valley. Where the path forks, ignore the branch climbing up to the dome of Pen y Bryn. Instead choose the LEFT FORK. This continues to drop gently through bracken until it eventually reaches a stile and gate.

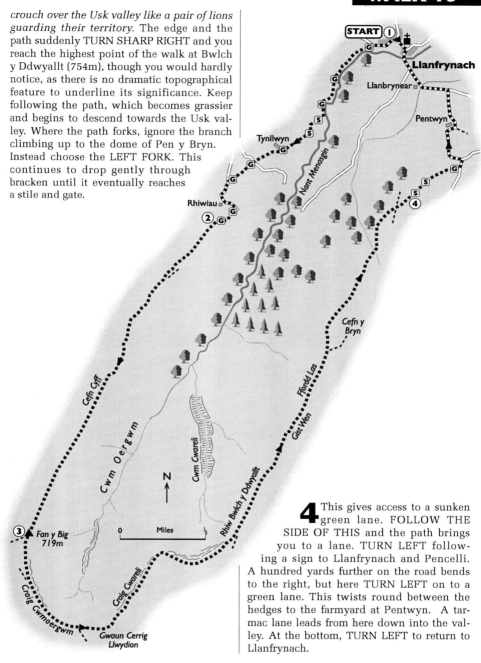

4 This gives access to a sunken green lane. FOLLOW THE SIDE OF THIS and the path brings you to a lane. TURN LEFT following a sign to Llanfrynach and Pencelli. A hundred yards further on the road bends to the right, but here TURN LEFT on to a green lane. This twists round between the hedges to the farmyard at Pentwyn. A tarmac lane leads from here down into the valley. At the bottom, TURN LEFT to return to Llanfrynach.

LLYN CWM LLWCH AND CORN DU

DESCRIPTION An expedition of great variety, with a range of alternatives to suit the mood or the weather. A charming woodland valley leads into the heart of the mountains. The path climbs to a mysterious cwm cradled in the rocky arms of the Beacons' highest crags. From here, a steep ascent leads directly to a high ridge leading on up to Corn Du. On the way, you pass an obelisk honouring one young boy who lost his way here and paid with his life. The whole route is 5½ miles, though it can be shortened by finishing at Llyn Cwm Llwch, or by avoiding the final ascent to Corn Du.

START Parking area at the end of the lane to Cwm Llwch. SO 006244.

DIRECTIONS Follow Ffrwdgrech Road from Brecon. This road starts about ½ mile towards the town centre from the western end of the Brecon by-pass where the A470 Cardiff road joins the A40 towards Llandovery. Ffrwdgrech Road leads southwards and you should keep on this lane for about 3 miles, ignoring side turnings to Cwmgwdi and elsewhere. The tarmac finishes at a gate. Go through this to the parking area on the grass beyond.

There is no public transport near this route.

I It's very tempting to linger. This is a wonderful spot. Close-cropped grass borders a sparkling stream. Mature trees, harbouring melodious birdsong, neatly frame the dramatic backdrop of the Beacons' northern face. Just the place for a picnic, but perhaps later. The best is yet to come. FOLLOW THE TRACK AS IT CLIMBS GENTLY TOWARDS THE MOUNTAINS, accompanied by the clear tumbling waters of the Nant Cwm Llwch. When you reach some sheep pens and a cottage, FOLLOW THE WAY MARKS AROUND TO THE RIGHT of the property and climb two stiles to emerge into more open country. Ascend the grassy bank on a clear track. The gradient gradually steepens towards another stile that gives access to the open hillside and National Trust land. At a cairn, BEAR LEFT, heading into the heart of the cwm. Abruptly, Llyn Cwm Llwch appears at your feet, concealed until the last moment in a rocky amphitheatre. *The lake is a mysterious legacy of glacial erosion and lies embraced in the mighty arms of Pen y Fan and Corn Du. You may see tiny figures toiling up the great ridge of Corn Du above.*

2 There is a big sandstone rock where the track arrives at the water. *Use this to rest, enjoy the view and savour the tranquillity of the mountain scene. A return to base from here will in itself be a great expedition. But if you are going any further you should be competent with a map and compass.* TO CONTINUE, CLIMB THE FAINT PATH IMMEDIATELY BEHIND THE SANDSTONE ROCK as it mounts a small spur. It soon becomes clearer and steeper. Further up the slope it becomes stone set and then joins up with the direct path you left at the cairn before Llyn Cwm Llwch. Keep climbing, now gaining the edge of the ridge and you will arrive at the Tommy Jones memorial, a small obelisk on the edge of the escarpment.

3 If you suddenly suffer from a shortage of enthusiasm or energy, or face the onset of poor weather, you can omit the ascent to Corn Du and descend from here by the return route. However, TO GAIN THE SUMMIT OF CORN DU, CONTINUE ON THE CLEAR PATH BEYOND THE MEMORIAL. This keeps near to the edge of the ridge and climbs directly to the summit of the Beacons' second in command.

4 The spectacular views from the sandstone cap will not disappoint, though mist can cloak the wide vista from the Black Mountain to Radnor Forest. Descend by the same path. At the Tommy Jones Memorial, continue along your outward route for about 150 yards only. LOOK CAREFULLY FOR A SMALLER PATH JUST TWO OR THREE YARDS TO THE LEFT OF YOUR ROUTE. There isn't exactly a junction and you will need to be observant, but it is clearly visible and represents the start of our alternative descent. Transfer across to it; if the weather is clear, your way is also easy to spot. Rather than dropping back towards Llyn Cwm Llwch, this narrower path follows a more level course around the edge of the escarpment. It soon descends gently around the edge, offering great views down into the cwm and further afield. *Brecon lies clearly ahead, and beyond the hills of mid Wales. You may be able to hear the faint 'boom' of artillery shells echoing from the vast wilderness of Mynydd Eppynt across the Usk valley.* A broader track joins from the left; this is the direct route from the Storey Arms. Continue on this as it descends the ridge of Pen Milan. As the ridge comes to its end, the route zig zags down and drops more gently through grass and gorse. The exact path is now not always easy to discern, but it doesn't matter. The open gorse clad hillside gradually tapers towards an apex where it meets enclosed land. This is where you need to reach.

5 Here a stile leads into a green lane. After about 100 yards, opposite a cottage, TURN RIGHT across a stile. Follow the path across a series of further stiles to rejoin our outward track near the parking area. Now, for that picnic!

The Tommy Jones Memorial

The grey stone monument is inscribed in memory of 5-year old Tommy Jones. He was walking with his father from Brecon station to his grandfather's farmhouse below the northern edge of the Beacons. By chance they met Tommy's grandfather and his 13-year-old cousin Willie a quarter of a mile from the house. Tommy and Willie were sent ahead to the house, but Tommy turned back, missed his way and somehow climbed up the Pen Milan ridge high into the mountains. His body was found nearly a month later. The inquest jurors used their fees to buy the memorial. Although over a century old it stands as a poignant reminder of tragedy.

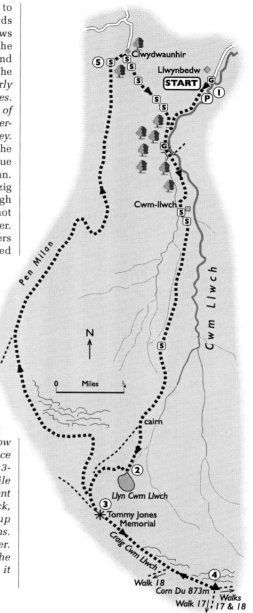

BEACONS HORSESHOE FROM THE SOUTH

DESCRIPTION This 6½-mile horseshoe of the headwaters of the Taf Fechan offers a superb ridge walk with spectacular views. The circuit includes the triumvirate of Corn Du, Pen y Fan, and Cribyn. There are two steep climbs, but most of the walk lies along the high ridges enclosing Blaen Taf Fechan. In good conditions, this is the best way to the top of the Beacons, **but it is a serious mountain expedition and can be confusing in mist and potentially dangerous in poor weather.**

START Lower Neuadd Reservoir. SO 032180. Larger parking areas also available at SO 037170 and at Pont Cwmyfedwen SO 043164.

DIRECTIONS The Neuadd reservoirs straddle the upper reaches of the Taf Fechan, in the heart of the Brecon Beacons. To reach here, take the minor road that crosses the Beacons between Talybont-on-Usk and Merthyr. This is a spectacular traverse in itself, linking the Taf Fechan and Caerfanell valleys to carve a route through the remote spine of the mountain massif. Although it is a high-level mountain route, there is a good road. A cul de sac leads north off it at a sharp bend, close to the head of Pentwyn reservoir (SO 047157). Follow this lane for about 2 miles until the tarmac ends by the old filter house near the reservoir dam.

There is no public transport near this route.

1 GO THROUGH THE GATE AT THE END OF THE ROAD AND FOLLOW THE NARROW PATH TO THE LEFT to reach the dam wall. *The walk starts as near to the heart of the mountains as you could hope to be. The grand triumvirate of Corn Du, Pen y Fan and Cribyn stretches out across the head of the valley, while to the left our first objective, the ridge of Graig Fan Ddu, looms up across the disused reservoir. This lower reservoir has now largely drained, but it was opened in* 1884 *to supply Merthyr with drinking water.* CROSS THE DAM WHERE A GATE LEADS ON TO THE OPEN HILLSIDE. The worst is first in terms of climbing! But working on the principle that it's best to get the steep work over early in the day, you'll soon be thankful for a clockwise route. Almost immediately after the gate there is a vague bifurcation. Ignore the right hand branch that continues past a wooden pole (though it is an alternative ascent). Instead, BEAR LEFT, crossing a small stream and climbing steadily and quite steeply up the slope next to a plantation. The steepest and rockiest section is towards the top, but soon you emerge suddenly on to the ridge. *Take a moment to look back across the Neuadd reservoirs. If the visibility is good, gaze across to the Sugar Loaf and Skirrid on the eastern horizon, guarding the approach from England. (See Kittiwake's **Walks on the Black Mountains** for routes on these hills near Abergavenny).*

2 TURN RIGHT and follow the path along the edge of the ridge. The way is clear and well defined. Gradients are gentle. But take care, especially in windy or slippery conditions, as the edge is precipitous. A cairn marks the alternative and rockier route up from Neuadd. Just over a mile along the ridge, another cairn just to the left of the path signals a narrower section of ridge known as Rhiw yr Ysgyfarnog. *In good weather, westward views open up across the Black Mountain of Carmarthenshire and as far as the Gower. In mist, progress is featureless but the route is clear.* Eventually the ridge curves right around the head of the Taf Fechan valley and drops slightly to the col at Bwlch Duwynt. Here is a major junction of paths.

3 The direct route from Storey Arms on the A470 joins from the left (**Walk 18**). A right fork provides a direct path to Pen y Fan, avoiding Corn Du. But having come so far, it seems a pity to miss the short ascent up the latter's impressive rocky cone, so CONTINUE AHEAD up the stony steps to conquer the sandstone buttress of the Beacons' second highest peak.

4 From the top of Corn Du FOLLOW THE ROCKY PATH ALMOST EXACTLY DUE

EAST (90°) from the summit. Use a compass in misty weather. This descends a short way to the pass and then rises to the summit of Pen y Fan.

5 Leave the summit across the sloping plateau heading towards our third peak, Cribyn. In mist check your direction using a compass and a bearing of 150°. At the end of the plateau the descent becomes steep and rocky, though steps both reduce the effects of erosion and ease progress. Near the bottom, the path divides. Straight ahead lies the Cribyn 'avoiding route'. This is a tempting option with the steep pyramid ahead of you. And it could prove useful if time is short. Otherwise, maintain your resolve and BEAR LEFT to follow the ridge path down to the bwlch. From here it is a steady slog up Cribyn's summit cone, though a well-made path helps. Once at the top, the route taken seems tame compared to the horrors of the north ridge on your left. *Take care on the summit, for there are steep drops*. FOLLOW THE PATH ON A BEARING OF ABOUT 150° and descend reasonably gently on a clear path. The gradient steepens as you approach Bwlch ar y Fan, more generally known in English as 'The Gap'. *The justification for this nomenclature and the prefixed definite article is clear. This is a key natural break in the highest ground of the Beacons. The Taf Fechan and Nant Cynwyn almost join, providing a course for the gently graded path that crosses the watershed between the southern valleys and Brecon. This is an ancient route; the site of a Roman road.*

6 TURN RIGHT to follow the course of the Roman road southwards through a gate and continue descending gently towards Neuadd reservoirs. As you approach the lower reservoir, the track is forced to TURN RIGHT in front of a gully blocked by a landslide. From here it leads directly and quickly back down to the starting point.

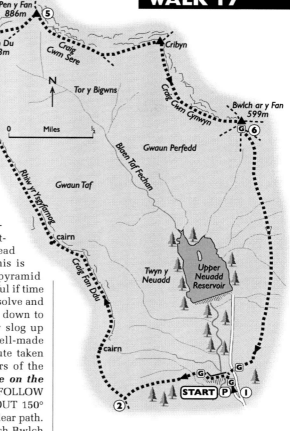

Pen y Fan

*At 886m (2960 feet) this is the highest point in Britain south of Snowdonia. Much of the highest land is in the care of the National Trust; Eagle Star Insurance gifted this area to the Trust in 1965. The wide panorama confirms the topographical significance of this rocky summit. Northwards, the eye is drawn across the broad pastoral acres of the Wye Valley to the rolling hills of mid Wales. Eastwards, Llangorse Lake (**Walk 1**) shimmers at the foot of the Black Mountains. To the west the vast wilderness of Fforest Fawr and the Black Mountain stretches towards the sea. Southwards lie the coal and iron valleys of South Wales reaching down to the Bristol Channel. Far below, Llyn Cwm Llwch lies in a deep glacial hollow (see **Walk 16**).*

THE BEACONS FROM STOREY ARMS

DESCRIPTION This is the quickest and easiest way up to the two highest summits of the Brecon Beacons. It is also the most popular, so it is busy on weekends. Nevertheless, it is a satisfying and interesting ascent on good, well-made paths. Because of this, navigation is relatively easy. But this is still a serious mountain expedition. The weather can be very different on the top and on a cold misty day you could be a million miles from the main north-south Wales trunk road rather than just two and a half. So take the usual precautions and make sure you can use a compass.

START Lay-by ½ mile south of the Storey Arms, on the A470 mid way between Brecon and Merthyr. SN 987199.

DIRECTIONS A substantial off-road lay-by crowns the summit of the A470 between Cardiff and Merthyr, just a few hundred yards south of the Storey Arms. There is free parking, though it gets busy on weekends and at bank holidays. There are toilets here and often a mobile catering van.

Service X43 (Cardiff-Merthyr-Brecon-Abergavenny) and 742 (Aberdare–Brecon) runs past the Storey Arms (Monday–Saturday). On summer Sundays and bank holidays, Beacons Bus serves the start.

I WALK NORTH through the lay by and then continue on along the verge of the main road, until you reach the Storey Arms. *This is not a pub but was once a youth hostel and is now an outdoor centre owned by Cardiff Council. However, other refreshment opportunities are usually available in various lay bys on this stretch of road, offering the usual variety of fried sandwiches and drinks.* Immediately after the Storey Arms, TURN RIGHT by a red phone box and follow a sign to cross a stile.

2 A well-constructed stone path climbs up from the Storey Arms. This combats erosion caused by the feet of many thousands of walkers. It also makes the going relatively easy all the way round. *Soon there are views down the Taf Fawr valley, with the three reservoirs serving Cardiff's aqueous needs. As you come to the top of a shoulder of land, the flat summit plateau of Corn Du comes into view, perched like a hat on the horizon.* A short descent is now required to cross the very highest reaches of Cardiff's river at Blaen Taf Fawr.

3 Stepping-stones cross the stream and then the climb begins in earnest. It's a well graded route, with excellent views and not unreasonably steep. As you near the summit cone, the path up from Llyn Cwm Llwch merges from the left (see **Walk 16**). The final ascent is steeper and the path is right by the edge of the escarpment. *There's a good view down into the glacial hollow of Llyn Cwm Llwch and you can see the Tommy Jones memorial obelisk further down the ridge (see* **Walk 16**). A final rocky section leads to the summit of Corn Du.

4 From the top of Corn Du, it is possible to miss out the second summit, Pen y Fan, by following the path south from the summit to Bwlch Duwynt. This may be useful if time is short. But it is just a short way on to the final goal and it would be a shame not to complete the walk if all is well. To reach Pen y Fan, take the path east (90°) from the summit. It soon descends and curves round in an east northeasterly direction, quickly reaching the bwlch between the two highest beacons. A short ascent brings you to the summit of the National Park, Pen y Fan, at 886 metres.

5 *This is higher than anywhere in Wales (outside Snowdonia), or in England (outside Cumbria). So you can expect a fine view on a clear day, though you would be unwise to take a clear day for granted! The panorama is extensive. South, over the old coal and iron valleys of South Wales and out across the Bristol Channel to the purple haze of Exmoor. The island of Steep Holme rises in the middle of the Severn Sea. Northwards, the eye is drawn over the Usk and Wye catchments to Radnor Forest, and the Clee Hills of southern Shropshire. West and north-*

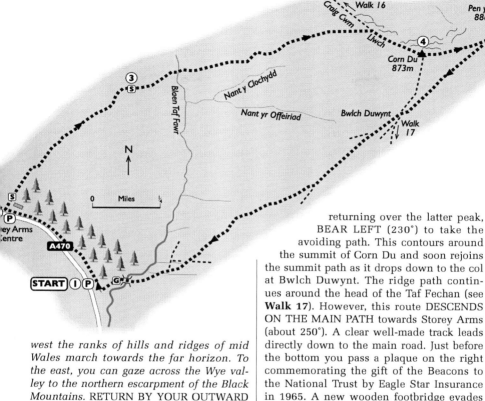

west the ranks of hills and ridges of mid Wales march towards the far horizon. To the east, you can gaze across the Wye valley to the northern escarpment of the Black Mountains. RETURN BY YOUR OUTWARD ROUTE (about 220°) to the lowest point between Pen y Fan and Corn Du. Instead of returning over the latter peak, BEAR LEFT (230°) to take the avoiding path. This contours around the summit of Corn Du and soon rejoins the summit path as it drops down to the col at Bwlch Duwynt. The ridge path continues around the head of the Taf Fechan (see **Walk 17**). However, this route DESCENDS ON THE MAIN PATH towards Storey Arms (about 250°). A clear well-made track leads directly down to the main road. Just before the bottom you pass a plaque on the right commemorating the gift of the Beacons to the National Trust by Eagle Star Insurance in 1965. A new wooden footbridge evades the stepping-stones and a gate leads through a patch of woodland back to the lay by.

Corn Du

CRAIG CERRIG-GLEISIAD AND FAN FRYNYCH

DESCRIPTION An exciting and interesting circuit of a classic glacial cwm, carved by ice, colonised by Iron Age dwellers, medieval farmers and rare alpine plants. At three miles, this is one of the shortest walks in the book. But it is also one of the most demanding. It climbs directly through the secretive cwm and along the top of a dramatic rocky escarpment. It requires care and is best avoided altogether in high wind or icy conditions. There is a steep and loose descent.

START Lay-by and picnic site on northbound side of A470, SN 971223.

DIRECTIONS To reach the start, take the A470 from either Brecon or Merthyr. There is a lay-by about 1½ m north of the Storey Arms. Bus X43 (Abergavenny – Brecon – Merthyr) and 742 (Brecon – Aberdare) operate along this road Monday to Saturday. The nearest stop is by Llwyn Celyn youth hostel, a short way north of the start. Beacons Bus also passes here on summer Sundays and bank holidays.

1 GO THROUGH THE KISSING GATE signed to Twyn Dylluan Du and Forest Lodge. Climb a well-made path up through woodlands just above a stream. At the wall, go through the gap next to the gate. Continue STRAIGHT AHEAD towards the amphitheatre of cliffs, next to the stream. *You've entered another world. The traffic noise has abated and the main road is completely out of view. Trees cling precariously to the precipitous rocky crags that surround the hidden bowl. Below, heather and ferns carpet the ground and a lovely grassy path takes you up into the cwm.* Further up a sign asks you to BEAR LEFT to avoid an eroded mound. *This is glacial moraine, capped by the site of an Iron Age settlement. This area has been used for centuries as summer pasture. There are remains of fields and house platforms from the Middle Ages when farmers lived here*

with their stock during the summer months. The path circumnavigates the mound and then climbs more steeply up the escarpment. Just below the brow, a white way mark indicates a path left. Follow this as it rises gently and arrives at a gate in the ridge fence.

2 To visit the top of Fan Frynych, TURN RIGHT here and follow the broad track. It rises gently to the summit plateau with fine views across Brecon and on to the northern profile of the Black Mountains. Pen y Fan and Corn Du dominate the eastern horizon across Glyn Tarell. At the highest point of the ridge, you reach an area of hollows. The trig point, a white concrete pillar, lies about 200 yards to the LEFT of the track and is reached by a small path. This could be confusing in mist so if in doubt stay on the track. On a clear day the detour is worth it for the views westwards.

3 From the summit RETRACE YOUR STEPS to point 2, where you gained the ridge. CONTINUE ON AHEAD with the fence on your left to a shallow depression with a pond. Cross over two stiles and continue ahead on the path, this time with the fence on the right. Don't wander too far from the path, as there are steep cliffs on your left. The path climbs up to the top of Craig Cerrig-gleisiad.

4 It then curves round the top of the precipice with good views down into the cwm. *Take care here as there is no fence on the edge. The descent also requires great caution. It is steep and often slippery. You will probably need to use hands and feet and certainly take your time.* The path brings you to the bottom of the cwm at the gate. Return down the path to the car park.

Craig Cerrig-gleisiad and Fan Frynych National Nature Reserve

This spectacular reserve covers two great rocky amphitheatres created by the last ice age. You encircle Craig Cerrig-gleisiad on this walk. (Craig Cwm-du and the summit of Fan Frynych are visited on Walk 20 from the National Park Mountain Centre.) Around twenty thousand years ago a glacier

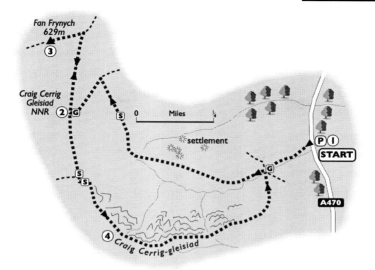

carved out the 500-foot cliffs. As the climate warmed, the retreating ice left rocks behind in the hollowed-out cwms. These moraines, now covered by grass, are the humps and bumps you can see today.

Craig Cerrig-gleisiad is north facing and reaches a height of over 600 metres above sea level. It therefore provides the southernmost British habitat for mountain plants such as purple saxifrage and mossy saxifrage. These arctic species do not occur again until the Alps. You may also see wild ponies and Welsh Black cattle.

Fan Frynych

FAN FRYNYCH AND CRAIG CWM-DU

DESCRIPTION Fan Frynych dominates the view southwards from the Mountain Centre. Its shapely profile marks the northernmost ridge of Fforest Fawr, the vast area of moorland west of the upper Taf. Its most impressive features are the two north-facing precipitous crags of Craig Cerrig-gleisiad and Craig Cwm-du. The former is visited on **Walk 19**. Craig Cwm-du, the highlight of this walk, is a remote and isolated cwm, colonised by alpine plants and visited by the red kite. The whole area from point 2 is included in a national nature reserve. The outward route of this 6½-mile walk lies over the main ridge of Fan Frynych, culminating in a descent to Craig Cwm-du. In mist this part of the walk requires careful navigation and competent use of a compass. The return is along an easy and clear track following the base of the ridge and overlooking the Usk and Senni valleys.

START Brecon Beacons National Park Mountain Centre. SN977263.

DIRECTIONS The Mountain Centre is signposted along a lane from Libanus, on the A470 Brecon-Merthyr road. It is about 1½ miles from the turning. You can also reach it from the A4215 road from Sennybridge.

Beacons Bus serves the mountain centre on summer Sundays and bank holidays. The nearest weekday public transport is the X43, which travels along the A470. The centre is around a mile from here.

I TURN LEFT out of the Mountain Centre car park and follow the road 200 yards to a T-junction. Go straight across following a track over the common, with a wood on the left and the bulk of Fan Frynych ahead of you. At the end of the common, you join a farm access track, which leads to a road. GO STRAIGHT ACROSS THE ROAD, following a lane signposted to Forest Lodge. In just over half a mile, where the tarmac lane turns sharp right to a group of buildings, CONTINUE STRAIGHT AHEAD along a stony track with a wood on your right. About half-a-mile further, cross a cattle grid and go through a gate.

2 TURN LEFT here. A signpost a little way back from the junction indicates the route to the A470 and Llwyn-y-celyn youth hostel. The track heads directly towards the hillside and at its base passes the entry sign to Craig Cerrig-gleisiad national nature reserve. The route bears left here to slant diagonally up the side of the hill. As it gains the crest of the hill, TURN SHARP RIGHT to stay on the main track. This now climbs steadily up the nape of the ridge. *There are good views left across Glyn Tarell, with the A470 snaking up to the Storey Arms. The flat caps of Corn Du and Pen-y-fan dominate the scene. Take a moment to look behind and enjoy the panorama over Brecon to the Black Mountains and beyond.* As you reach the highest point of the ridge, take care to look out for the white painted trig point, set back about 200 yards to the right of the track. A path TURNS RIGHT off the main track to reach this, but in mist you will need to take care to spot this. If you find the main track is starting to descend, you have gone too far. The OS column marks the highest point of Fan Frynych at 629 metres. The view now extends westwards to the Black Mountain. *You can also see the two great crags of Craig Cerrig-gleisiad (**Walk 19**) and Craig Cwm-du, peeping over the wide moorland horizon.*

3 Continue straight ahead from the summit (bearing 250°), following the broad and rather squelchy track across the grassy plateau. Gradually descend for about half a mile.

4 Watch out for a well-made stone cairn standing just a few yards to the left of the path. This is the marker for the diverging route to Craig Cwm-du. *If you want to shorten the walk, the main track ahead winds on down to point **6**.* However, to follow the complete route, TURN LEFT (205°) on to a narrower but initially clear path past the cairn. This descends gently at first, but soon becomes much steeper; it is also less evident on the ground. However, if you maintain this direction, you will drop down to the upper reaches of Nant Cwm-du, reaching a small stream deep in the defile. TURN RIGHT and follow the stream downhill. The small path becomes broader and crosses and re-crosses the water with the aid of a couple of new footbridges. *To the left the towering crags of Craig Cwm-du stretch up to the sky, trees clinging to the vertiginous slopes. Reaching the heart of the cwm, you realise what a very special place this is, and the chances are you will have it all to yourself.*

5 *The path comes to a T-junction with a wider track. Just a few yards to the left this track gains the ancient Roman road of Sarn Helen, climbing between Fan Nedd and Fan Llia on its way to the garrison fortress at Neath (**Walk 14** covers part of the Roman road further south).* However, we TURN RIGHT here. The stony track rises slight-

ly and curves round the western flank of Fan Frynych, with pretty views across Heol Senni.

6 Continue straight head as a track joins from the right. This is the direct (shorter) route from Fan Frynych's summit that diverged at point **4**. The walk now continues along a shelf of rough pasture between the rising bulk of the mountain and the valley

below. You rejoin the outward route at point **2**, continuing back to the Mountain Centre by the outward course.

Craig Cwm-du

Craig Cwm-du is part of the National Nature Reserve covering the whole of Fan Frynych. The array of spectacular cliffs shelters an isolated and remote cwm, origin of a minor tributary of the Senni. The trees and shrubs clinging to the cliffs make this an unusual habitat and the crags are known for their Welsh poppies. About 80 species of birds have been seen in the whole reserve area, and this wild corner is a good place to see red kites and other raptors wheeling overhead.

Sensible precautions

OS Explorer map 12 covers most of the walks; the remainder (**1, 7 & 9**) are on Explorer 13. Always wear walking boots and be prepared to use a compass or GPS equipment. Tell someone where you are going and stick to your route. **Never** be too proud to turn back. The mountains will be here tomorrow. *Make sure you are too.*

   Details of access by public transport to the start of each walk have been included. The nearest railway stations are Abergavenny and Merthyr. A regular bus service (X43) runs right through the heart of the park from Abergavenny to Merthyr via Brecon, though there is no Sunday service. The National Park organises a network of services on Sundays and bank holidays in summer. Only walks **14, 16** and **17** are impossible to reach by public transport, though **3, 4, 8** and **20** are only served on Sundays. For details of public transport contact Traveline Cymru (www.traveline-cymru.org or 0870 608 2 608).

KEY TO THE MAPS

——	Main road
═══	Minor road
▬►▬	Walk route and direction
①	Walk instruction
– – –	Path
⌒⌒	River/stream
Ⓖ	Gate
Ⓢ	Stile
△	Summit
🌲🌳	Woods
🍺	Pub
Ⓟ	Parking

THE COUNTRYSIDE CODE

- Be safe – plan ahead and follow any signs
- Leave gates and property as you find them
- Protect plants and animals, and take your litter home
- Keep dogs under close control
- Consider other people

The CroW Act 2000, implemented throughout Wales in May 2005, introduced new legal rights of access for walkers to designated open country, predominantly mountain, moor, heath or down, plus all registered common land. This access can be subject to restrictions and closure for land management or safety reasons for up to 28 days a year.

Published by
Kittiwake
3 Glantwymyn Village Workshops, Glantwymyn, Machynlleth, Montgomeryshire SY20 8LY

© Text & map research: Alastair Ross 2008
© Maps & illustrations: Kittiwake 2008
Drawings by Morag Perrott

Cover photos: *Main* – Beacons from Cwm Llwch.
Inset – Vaynor Church. *Alastair Ross*

Printed by MWL, Pontypool.

ISBN: **978 1 902302 57 7**